BLACK HISTORY SHOULD BE TAUGHT 365 DAYS A YEAR

BLACK HISTORY SHOULD BE TAUGHT 365 DAYS A YEAR

JASPER CEPHUS

Library of Congress Control Number:		2021911616
ISBN:	Hardcover	978-1-6641-7923-3
	Softcover	978-1-6641-7922-6
	eBook	978-1-6641-7921-9

Print information available on the last page.

Rev. date: 06/07/2021

To order additional copies of this book, contact:
Xlibris
844-714-8691
www.Xlibris.com
Orders@Xlibris.com
825976

CONTENTS

AFRICAN CIVILIZATION OF ANCIENT AMERICA

One of the most important aspects of Black istory worldwide is the development of Black civilization because of the early and persistent use and application of trade and commerce. Because of such early and well-organized trading and commercial systems throughout the prehistoric Black world, Blacks were able to move throughout the world and establish one of the world's first cultures and civilizations. Although it is said that Black migrated from the original homeland of mankind in Africa to settle all in Asia, Europe, Australia, and the Americas (see *Scientific American*, September 2000, pp. 80-87; this is a recent publication), long before differentiation of the races from the original Nigritic to Nigritic, Caucasoid, mongoloid, along with the various mixed races, such as Polynesians, Native Americans, Japanese, Malays, Mediterranean, Whites, East Indians (the mixed Negroid Caucasian type, not the pure Black pre-Aryan Nigritic Indians), Arabs, Latinos (mestizos, mullatoes, zambos, Spaniards), and a number of other mixed races and regional types, the purpose of the early migrations of Blacks from Africa to the rest of the world was not merely following and hunting wild animals, as some theorists have claimed, but searching for commodities, like red ochre to paint the smooth, dark skin from insects and decoration. Another purpose for the early migrations of Africans to other parts of the world was to establish trading and commercial links to those of their own people, who had left previously. Hence, even if the earliest migrations were after wandering herds of animals, further migrations were in search of links with their kinsmen and women.

AFRICA GAVE EUROPE THEIR FIRST CIVILIZATION

Ancient Crete civilization existed from 1200 to 300 BC.

Unfortunately, one cannot use the Bible today as a historical reference; the good book has been contaminated with false pretends with the intention to explain away truth and facts (Suzar, *Blacked Out through Whitewash*. Greek, the Black of Europe, is the first civilization built in Europe; supporting facts are Black sculptures and archeologist finds. Egyptians, Libyans, and the Phoenicians are all Black people. All three had access to travel by ships to Aegean and Crete of Greece. They transported math, geometry, and algebra to build the civilization in Greece. The black statuettes, figurines, and circular type of tomb and architecture in building structures and the Minoan were ancient Crete attinitive of Libyan, and Africa. All were found by archeologists.

Examples are the use of the simple wooden bows, and the chisel edge arrows for bring down birds and small deer, the flexible ox-hide shield for hunting big game as well as for war. Theoo fine craftsman ship and characteristic forms of vessels in hard wood, the peculiar vessels of cooper with no neck or rim, but a trough spout inserted in the shoulder. Common also to the early men of Egypt, Libya, and Crete (Crete of

Greek) at all events associated in Egypt with other Libyan connections--are the lock of hair left on one side of the head, the narrow- pointed beard and the peculiar lion cloth and protective belt; common like wise to the women, costumes variously elaborated from a blanket-like wrapper, open down the front from neck, and folded over itself from waist, quite different, therefore, from the apron-shawl of primitive Babylonia. Much of these were confirmed by the British archaeologist John Pendelbury who made excavations in Crete.

The African influence in Greek culture did not end with the Libyan arrivals in the Messara. They continued into the old kingdom or pyramid age: Old kingdom Egypt was at a different level of sociopolitical development from pre-palatial Crete. Old kingdom Egypt can be characterized as a state society ruled by a powerful political and economic elite presided over by the king. Through Egypt, there was a flourishing literate bureaucracy and centralized control over the procurement of raw materials and their redistribution and over craft specialization. Crete were characterized as an egalitarian village community. The main trade could be identified: raw material, exchange of finished luxury goods. There were evidence of the transmission of technologies and esoteric knowledge, and these reflect interaction between a developing societies and Egypt. Base on the survival of archaeological material, Crete was located just south of Greece; after a volcanic eruption, Crete was destroyed. It is from that period onward that Crete civilization began to spread under the control of Greece and eventually the Roman Empire.

AFRICA: THE LARGEST AND THE WORLD'S RICHEST EMPIRE

Sonni Ali was the founder and first emperor of the Songhai or Songhay. This empire occupied the rich tract of land within the buckle of the Majestic River, Niger. When the Mali Empire weakened, Sonni Ali took advantage of this and led his infantry and cavalry to victory, effectively conquering major centers for commerce and culture like Timbuktu, while simultaneously building a fleet to protect the Niger River, which was so vital to their survival. During his reign, the Songhai Empire had become the largest empire in the history of Africa. After six years of fighting, the city of Djenne also succumbed to Sonni Ali's tactics. Because the king of Djenne surrendered, the city was spared any major punishment, and Sonni Ali went on to conqueror the land between Djenne and Timbuktu and beyond.

Sonni Ali, also known as Sonni Ali Ber, was born Ali Kolon, died 1492.

BLACK AFRICAN SPHINX

We all have seen the damage done to the faces of the Sphinxes of Giza or all the statures in Africa. Some nose and lips on ancient Egyptian statures of Sphinxes knocked off because of collective or individual racist intent. Once the statures of Sphinxes were defaced, you will find the restoration of the statures of Sphinxes with pointed long nose and thin lips and blue eyes. In addition to defacing, the color of the statures of Sphinxes will be changed, intentionally, from black to light brown or yellow. With the rise of White racism, which real aim was to justify the enslavement of the Black people, certain noted scholars denied that the Egyptians of Black Africa were White people.

The Catholic religion stole, robbed the books of the Bible, tried to destroy Black African culture and history through whitewash (Suzar), with the intent that everything created and found by the human race was white. Lol, White and Black people go to school for twelve years to learn that we are living in an all-White world.

BLACK HISTORY SHOULD BE TAUGHT 365 DAYS A YEAR

African history should be taught 365 days a year, intended to capture the attention of the world, open the minds of so many people who have been lied to, misled, and deceived by use of blacked out and whitewashed history. The amazing thing about it is the White people are still trying to deny or refuse to allow accountable evidence to be entertained in media and public schools. Though the history of Africa has been shipwrecked by White people, it is still ahead of Europe and Americas in historical resources. Africa was perpetuated in time, hundred thousand-plus years; they had great cities that were successful, they had kingdoms and empires, some of the great men and women who were the kings and queens still live in statues and carved in stones, etc. Were they sleeping in banana trees? Lol, yeah, you wish. Genetically, it have been proven that Black Africans are no part of a monkey, but genetically, the White people carry the ape gene. We are talking about the richest people in the world, the Africans. They were not dressed in tree leaves, but where are their palaces and artworks that will serve as reminders who the great Africans are? No matter how much the White people say that they made Africans better, historically, nothing the White people show that can equal the power, richness, education, scientific knowledge, and beauty that Africans had. Europe killed, robbed, burned, and destroyed the cities of Africa, blacked out through whitewash to hide the evidence of where the world got their civilizations from. After trying to obliterate statues, artifacts, and intelligence carved in stones in Africa, the White people overlooked the evidence in the Cuban Atlantic waters. There are pyramids and the Sphinx still found there, and an estimate of one hundred pyramids were built on the Mississippi River in USA, and the many cities built by Black Africans in the Americas include Cahokia and its pyramid in Illinois, USA. There are tunnels in Mississippi with intelligence on the walls, evidence put there by Black Africans but has been blacked out through whitewash.

Progressively, the truth is connecting the dots in the world, social, economic, and spiritual. People are learning where civilization began, why people readily adapt to fashion, music, taste of food, and accept the religion that have been found by the Black Africans maybe more than one hundred thousand years ago. Africa has been the provider of resources that fused the world economy for thousands of years.

AFRICANS CAME TO AMERICA

Recent discoveries in the field of linguistics and other methods have shown, without a doubt, that ancient Olmecs of Mexico, known as the Xi people, came originally from West Africa and were of the Mende African ethnic stock. According to Clyde A. Winters and other writers (see Clyde A. Winters website), the Mende script was discovered on some of the ancient Olmecs monuments of Mexico and were found to be identical to the very same script used by Mende people of West Africa. Although the carbon-14 testing date for the presence of the Black Olmecs or Xi people is about 1500 BC, journeys to Mexico and Southern USA may have come from West Africa much earlier, particularly around five thousand years before Christ. That conclusion is based on the discovery of an African native cotton in North America. It only possibleway of arriving where it was found, had to have been through human's hands. In that period in West Africa history and even before, civilization was in full bloom in West Sahara, what is known as Mauritania today. One of Africa's earlier civilizations, the Zingh Empire, existed and may have lived in what was a lake-filled wet and fertile Sahara, where ships crisscross from place to place.

BLACK AFRICANS IN AMERICAS THOUSANDS OF YEARS BEFORE THE WHITE PEOPLE

The term Olmec was coined by archeologists in reference to the Blacks who once inhabited the Olmecs sites. The word is derived from *olli* (rubber) because they traded in rubber. The Olmecs were known in Aztec myth-history as the people who lived in the direction of the rising sun. Several terms have been used throughout history that have often hidden Black African identity. Blacks have been called Moors, Numidians, Olmecs, Negroes, Canaanites, Jebusites, and so on. Comparisons have been made between the Olmecs' heads and a bust of King Taharqa. They look uncannily similar. Linguistically, there is evidence in support of the early African presence in Americas pointed out by scholars like Clyde Winters. The art of writing in the Americas originated in Africa. Albert Churchward has documented a number of strong similarities between the ancient Egyptians and other cultures in the Americas.

AFRICANS CREATED THE GUITAR

Africans invented and introduced the guitar to the world over four thousand years ago. Black African Moors brought the guitar to Spain and Egypt, then introduced the guitar to Greece. Now the guitar is found all over the world. The guitar have taken many shapes in the thousands of years; the guitar started from one string and progressively to numerous strings. The guitar took shape as a harp, tanbur, and lute, then the guitar was put into the piano. When the guitar was first invented, it was used as a medical instrument, by laying the one-string instrument on the chest of a patient and plucking the string until clogged, blocked circulation was opened up in the chest. People in the world as you know it today find therapy in guitar music.

AFRICANS MIGRATED TO ALL OVER THE WORLD

The migrations of Africans to all parts of the world occurred within the past hundred thousand years or more, before any other races existed. Thus, Black culture and civilization was being established when no other "races," as we know them today, existed. This is a fascinating historical event because having been *Homo sapiens* for over one hundred thousand years, it is very possible that Blacks could have gone through many periods of cultural development and civilization before the beginning of the Nile Valley civilization (since about 17,000 BC) or the Zingh civilization of the Southwestern Sahara (15,000 BC) or even Atlantis (10,000 BC) or the building of the Sphinx (7,000 BC). In fact, there is evidence from ancient East Indian chronicles (some of the pictures are on Africa American Web Ring (AAWR)) of the great scientific advancement of the Black prehistoric inhabitants of the Indus Valley civilization (6,000 BC-1,700 BC), who built flying machines, who had flushing toilets, cities on a grid-like pattern, and many of what we call modern conveniences.

WOOOOOW! About twenty thousand years ago, there was an aquatic civilization in the present-day dried-up Sahara Desert, where the Africans who lived on the edges of the inland sea built large ocean-going ships. Paintings of these ships can still be seen in the Sahara (and some appeared on *National Geographic* magazine about two years ago). For more on the aquatic civilizations of the prehistoric Sahara, see *African Presence in Early Asia* by Ivan Van Sertima and Runoko Rashidi, Transaction Publications, New Brunswick, New Jersey.

BLACK AFRICA RULED IN EUROPE FOR OVER 1,400 YEARS

Shocking, isn't it? It started with Septimius Severus and ended with the Moors (Moors are Black Africans).

Black rulership of the Roman Empire began in AD 193, with African-born Roman emperor Septimius Severus, a full-blooded African. Severus came from Leptis Magna, a thriving port with a fine natural harbor in what is now Libya, near Tripoli. He died on a Monday in AD 211.

There were four other Black emperors after Septimius Severus's dynasty. Often called the father of military strategy, Hannibal, another full-blooded African, performed the astounding feat of crossing the Alps on elephants in AD 218. With only twenty-six thousand of his original force of eighty-two thousand remaining, Hannibal defeated Rome, the mightiest military power of the age, which had a million men in every battle for the next fifteen years. His tactics are still taught in leading military academies of the United States, Europe, and other lands.

Black rulership was widespread in Europe during the Dark and Middle Ages.

The original "knights" were Black, including the knights of King Arthur's round table! That is why they were called knights, after the night or darkness of their skin.

An African king named Tormund ruled Ireland during the Anglo-Saxon period in England, reports the medieval historian Geoffrey of Monmouth.

ANCIENT AFRICANS IN CONGO AND UGANDA KNEW MATHEMATICS

The Ishango bones are the first evidence of a calculator in the world. Named after the place it was found in the Democratic Republic of Congo, the Ishango bone tools is the cradle of mathematics. It was said to date back as far as twenty-two thousand years, but previous existing civilizations of Africa suggest that the date could be over fifty thousand years.

It is a dark brown bone that happens to be the fibula of a baboon with a sharp piece of quartz affixed to the end for engraving. The first bone has been subject to a lot of interpretations at first. It was thought to be just a tally stick with a series of tally marks, but scientists have demonstrated that the grouping of notches on the bone is an indication of a mathematical understanding that goes beyond simple counting. In fact, many believed that the notches follow a mathematical succession. The notches have been interpreted as a prehistoric calculator. It is the oldest attestation of the practice of arithmetic in human history. A modern measurement tool copied from the bone tool is the slide ruler. Slide rulers became obsolete when electronic calculators hit the market. Electronic calculators use the same system in binary form of 0s and 1s.

ANCIENT BLACK CIVILIZATION THAT WAS NOT IN AFRICA

The Minoans, Ancient Greece

Archaeologist Manfred Bietak conducted extensive research on ancient Greek civilization and their connections to ancient Egypt. Bietak unearthed evidence from artwork as early as 7000 BC that depicts the early people inhabiting Greece were of African descent.

The Minoan culture of ancient Greece reached its peak at about 1600 BC. They were known for their vibrant cities, opulent palaces, and established trade connections. Minoan artwork is recognized as a major era of visual achievement in art history. Pottery, sculptures, and frescoes from the Minoan bronze age grace museum displays all over the world. Palace ruins indicate remnants of paved roads and piped water systems.

ANCIENT BLACK CIVILIZATION THAT WAS IN CHINA

Shang Dynasty of Ancient China

In a genetic study published in the *Proceedings of the National Academy of Sciences,* researchers found evidence showing the first African arrived in China about sixty thousand years ago. Researcher and population geneticist Li Jin states, "Our work shows that modern humans first came to southeast Asia and then moved later to northern China. This supports the idea that modern humans originated in Africa."

A 2009 published essay from *Light Words from the Dark Continent: A Collection of Essays* by Nibs Ra and Manu Amun offers insight to early Chinese civilizations. It states that first documented governance in China was headed by the Shang or Chiang Dynasty in 1500-1000 BC. King T'ang or Ta, founder of the Shang Dynasty, was of African descent. The Shang was also called Nakhi, which literally means "black man"; "black" (*na*) and "man" (*khi*). King T'ang and the Shang Dynasty were responsible for unifying China to form their first civilization.

ANCIENT BLACK CIVILIZATION THAT WAS NOT IN AFRICA

The Olmecs were an ancient civilization in the Americas. Researchers, such as Runoko Rashidi, Ivan Van Sertima, and Alexander von Wuthenau, have discovered and shared evidence showing that the original inhabitants of Mexico were of African descent. The Olmecs were no different from people found in the Mende regions of West Africa.

Best known for carving the colossal stone heads that date back to 1100 BC, more evidence of their existence before European explorers try to cover it up. The Olmecs built pyramid-like structure made of mud in Mexico. They were also very artistic and created terra-cotta art that displayed common activities like pottery. To add to their achievements, the Olmec people developed a calendar system around 3100 BC.

ANCIENT BLACK CIVILIZATION THAT WAS NOT IN AFRICA

Many scholars have concluded that the founders of the first Mesopotamian civilization were Black Sumerians. Mesopotamia was the biblical land of Shinar (Sumer), which sprang up around 3000 BC. After having the cuneiform script deciphered and researching ancient Mesopotamia for many years, Henry Rawlinson (1810-1895) discovered that the founders of the civilization were of Kushite (Cushite) origin. He made it clear that the Semitic speaker of Akkad and the non-Semitic speakers of Sumer were both Black people who called themselves *sag-gig-ga* or "black heads."

This was corroborated by other scholars, including Chandra Chakaberty, who asserted in his book *A*

Study in Hindu Social Polity that based on the statue and steles of Babylonia, the Sumerians were of dark complexion (chocolate color), short stature, but of sturdy frame, oval face, stout nose, straight hair, full head; they typically resembled the Dravidians. not only in cranium, but almost in all the details."

YOU ARE CHARACTERIZED

Black history is like a food, except it has no chemicals or cancer-causing agents. Black people getting white people MD,PHD etc. in white American schools, their first response would have a natural rejection of Black history. It is symbolized steadfast in a mental state, making it is difficult for the receiving containing of the mind to accept Black history and its culture.

Black history is flowing, but some educated Black Americans are following, trying to step in the White people's footprints, wanting to be like White people. Some will spend hundreds of dollars buying fur (wigs) in all colors to put on their head and trying to speak like White people, and if they are not blue Black, they will say they are mixed. There is no such thing as a mixed Black human. From the Black hue-man came all colors of people, brown-, dark-, black-skinned. They lack the knowledge that all hue-man beings can make people white, but white people cannot make hue-man beings. The above-described Black people are dangerous; they can be used by the White people to bring down Black humans all over the world. Those people, some are lawyers, but they didn't learn that the laws, science, math, geometry, trigonometry, algebra, speech, and religion came from Africa.

ANCIENT BLACK CIVILIZATION THAT WAS NOT IN AFRICA

Indus Kush Civilization

On March 3, 2000, historian Runoko Rashidi gave a lecture in Honolulu, Hawaii, about the presence of Black people in ancient and modern India. He stated that the face of India changed around 2000 BC, when nomadic Indo-Europeans or Aryans traveled to the Innis Valley and other fertile locations in Southern India. Prior to the invasion, Blacks in India built rich and advanced civilizations. Author Wayne Chandler recanted his amazing discoveries about Black people in ancient India in his book *African Presence in Early Asia*. The remarkable cities of Harappa and Mohenjo-Daro are only two of the many cities built by Black people. These cities cover large regions of modern-day India and modern-day Pakistan.

BLACK CIVILIZATION OF ANCIENT AMERICAS: PRIEST KING

The above ancient stone carving (500-1000 BC) of shamans of priest king clearly show distinct similarities in instruments held and purpose. The realistic carving of an African king and stone carving of a shaman from Columbia's San Agustin culture indicate diffusion of African religious practice to the Americas. In fact, the regions of Columbia and Panama of Americas were among the first places that Blacks were spotted by the first Spanish explorers to the Americas.

From the archaeological evidence gathered in West Africa and Mesoamericas, there is a reason to believe that African Negritics who found or influenced the Olmec civilization came from West Africa. Not only do Olmecs large stone heads resemble Black Africans from Ghana area, but also the ancient religious practices of the Olmec priest were similar to that of the West Africans', which included shamanism, the study of the Venus complex, which was part of the traditions of the Olmecs, as well as Ono and Dogon people of West Africa. The language connection is of significant importance since it has been found out through decipherment of the Olmec script that the ancient Olmec spoke the Mende language and wrote in the Mende script, which are still used in parts of West Africa and the Sahara to this day.

ANCIENT ARTISTIC FINE CRAFTSMANSHIP

An example of the sophisticated fine artistic craftsmanship done by Black Africans thousands of years before they taught the White Paleolithics in Europe speech, how to read and write, math, science, and hygiene's is a chair made for kings, used in religious ceremonies. The high slightly-curved back is fixed to a stool with crossed legs. The wood is partially gold-plated and inlaid with semiprecious stones, glass paste, glazed terra-cotta, ebony, and ivory. Artworks like this were robbed from the Valley of the Kings graves of Africans by the White Paleolithics of Europe.

ANCIENT TECHNOLOGY IN TODAY'S SOCIETY

The hue-mans gave life and structure to the White people. We gave the White people everything they have right now. We gave them knowledge on the pyramid on the USA dollar bills. We gave them maths: trigonometry, geometry, algebra; science; religion; and speech. The White people learned the knowledge on the "third eye," identified on the pyramid, from the great intellect of Black Africans. The intention of white power structure was to whitewash and destroy evidence showing that this knowledge came from Africa.

ANTHROPOLOGISTS VERIFY THERE WAS AN ANCIENT BLACK PRESENCE IN THE AMERICAS

During the International Congress of American Anthropologists held in Barcelona, Spain, in 1964, a French anthropologist pointed out that all that was missing to prove a definite presence of Black African people in the Americas before the White people were the Black African skeletons, to add to the already-found Black African-featured terra-cotta. Later, in February 1975, skeletons of Black African people dating to 1200s were found at a pre-White people grave in the Virgin Islands. Andrel Wierzynski, a Polish craniologist, also concluded, based on his study of skeletons, that skulls of Black African people were found in Mexico.

Based on the many finds for a Black African people presence in ancient Mexico, some of the most enthusiastic proponents of a pre-White people Black African presence in Mexico are Mexican professionals. They conclude that Black Africans must have established early important trading centers on the coasts along Vera Cruz, from which Middle America's first civilization grew.

In retrospect, from as early as about 100,000 BC, ancient Black Africans did visit the Americas, where they stayed for tens of thousands of years. By 30,000 BC to about 15,000 BC, a massive migration from the Sahara toward the Indian Ocean and the Pacific in the east occurred from the Sahara. Black Africans also migrated westward across the Atlantic Ocean toward the Americas during that period until the very eve of Columbus's first journey to the Americas.

BENIN CITY IN NIGERIA OF AFRICA

picture from google.com/globalsecurity.org

Benin City is the capital of Edo State, south of Nigeria. In Central Kings Square, the Benin City National Museum traces the history of Benin Empire. It also has the displays of terra cotta sculpture. Oba's Palace has the beauty of bronze plaques historically decorated the walls, also indicating historical events and life at court. Walter Rodney wrote at the end of the thirteenth century that the town seem to be very great, and when you make your way into it, you will see a great wide street that is not paved, which seems to be seven or more times wider than the Wamoes Street in Amsterdam, the oldest street in Amsterdam. The king's palace is a group of buildings that occupies as much space as the town of

Harlem, (New York City, USA. Harlem area= 1.4 miles squared = est. 54,641,664 square feet's) and which is surrounded with walls. The town is composed of thirty main streets, very straight and 120 feet wide. It has infinite small intersecting streets. The houses are close together, arranged in good order.

The fascinating Benin City walls extend for 16,000 kilometers in all, colored pieces of inlaid stone of more than five hundred interconnected settlement boundaries. They cover 6,500 square kilometers, and all dug by the Edo people. The measurements are four times longer than the Great Wall of China and used a hundred times more materials than the Great Pyramid of Cheops, Egypt, of Africa's last seven wonders of the world. It is said to have taken 150 million hours of digging to construct and the largest only archaeological occurrence on this earth.

The beautiful Benin City of Nigeria in Africa was destroyed, robbed, and burned to ashes by the British forces under Admiral Harry Rawson in 1897.

BENJAMIN BANNEKER

Benjamin Banneker was a free African American, self-educated mathematician, scientist, surveyor, almanac author, and farmer. In 1753, at age twenty-two, Banneker completed a wooden clock that stroked on the hour. The same make a model is in London today; it is called the Big Ben. In 1791, Banneker teamed up with Major Andrew Ellicott and mapped the new Washington Capital of USA, today known as Washington DC. Upon Major Ellicott's absence, Banneker completed the project by himself. Benjamin Banneker was an active writer of almanac and studied astronomy by watching the stars and moon. Benjamin Banneker was born on November 9, 1731, and died on October 25, 1806.

BLACK AFRICAN QUEEN OF EGYPT, CLEOPATRA

Cleopatra, the seventh queen of Egypt of Black Africa, has come down to us through twenty centuries as the perfect example of a seductive woman. With her Black beauty, learning, and culture, she fascinated and held two successive masters of the world. The first was Julius Caesar. He was debonair, elegant in manners and movement, a great swimmer, a swordman, a beloved ruler, and able orator. The second was Caesar's friend and successor Mark Anthony. He was tall, well built, with muscles of a gladiator, generous, impulsive, and a bon vivant. He was a matchless orator, of whom it was said, "There was no man of his time like him for addressing a multitude or for carrying soldiers with him by the force of his word."

Such were the two giants Cleopatra enslaved. She, on her side, if not the most beautiful woman of her time, was perhaps the most captivating, learned, and most witty. It is said that she spoke Egyptian, Latin, Ehtiopian, Hebrew, Arabic, Syrian, fluently as well in several African dialects.

BLACK AFRICAN PYRAMID (MOUND) IN USA

Cahokia is a city built by Black Africans thousands of years before the coming of the White race. White-controlled media is still trying to explain away the existence of Black Africans. They use false characters of pictures on the Internet to hide the facts about Cahokia, intending White and Black people not to look any further than their 20/20 vision can focus upon, a knowledge filter choosing what you will see. Fortunately, modern science have proved, by test done on skeletons exhumed from Cahokia grave sites, that their DNA is of Black Africans who occupied and built Cahokia, its city and pyramid (mound).

The Olmecs seem to be the oldest Black Africans existed in Americas, thousands of years before the White people. Olmecs were the first in Americas to do writing. The mound builders were Blacks. The truth about the mound is suppressed because they were an advanced civilization of woolly-haired Black people who was indigenous (native) to North America, kin to the Olmecs of South America. The site where the pyramid was built is in Cahokia, Illinois, USA. It was the largest city in USA until 1800s. There are pyramids in Mexico identified by its architecture and culture that they were built by Black Africans of Egypt. The mound has the same architectural design that the Egyptians of Africa has. While Whites were trying to hide and explain away truth and facts about Blacks in North America, a deteriorated pyramid (whites called a mound) was the largest pyramid in the world, built by Black Africans. Many terms have been used by Whites throughout Black history that have often hidden Blacks' identity. Black African religious and cultural traditions permeated Aztec and Mayan civilizations.

BLACK QUEEN AMANIRENAS

Amanirenas was a queen of the Meroitic kingdom of Kush. She reigned from about 40 BCE-10 BCE in Northeast Africa. When Roman Emperor Augustus levied a tax on the Kushites, Amanirenas and her son Akinidad led a fierce attack on a Roman fort at the Egyptian city Aswan. Amanirenas looted the city of Roman's possession, taking the statues, head of Augustus. She carried the head back to Kush and buried it under the ground so her people could walk over it. Under orders from Augustus, the Roman general Petronius, holding the office of Roman prefect in Egypt, retaliated but met a strong resistance from Amanirenas and her troops but pushed Amanirenas's armies back out. According to a detailed report made by Strabo (17:53-54), the Roman troops advanced far into Kush and finally reached Napata. Although they withdrew again to the north, they left behind a garrison in Qasr Ibrim (Primis), which now became the border of the Roman Empire. Kushites made a renewed attempt to seize Primis, but Petronius's resistance was drawing weak. What is hidden in all White people history about Black people is that White people are losers, but they make it look like they won. Amanirenas received the support of surrounding nations in the fight against Augustus's army, and Amanirenas's bittersweet victory was hers. Marching at the head of her army, Amanirenas reached the strategic city of Qasr Ibrim, south of Egyptian city of Aswan.

Rome, exhausted in their war against Amanirenas, decided to negotiate a peace term. Augustus was willing to lay aside the arms if Amenirenas would negotiate a settlement with him. The Candace (Amenirenas) agree. She sent her ambassadors to the Greek island of Samos to meet with representatives of Rome. They negotiated the return of all conquered lands and the remission of the controversial tax. Rome historian Strabo recorded the result of the meeting: Amanirenas's victory established her as the first Black queen of Africa.

BLACK AFRICANS CROSS THE PACIFIC TO AMERICA

Ancient vessels were loaded with all types of trade goods, and not only did they crisscross the Atlantic, but they also traded out in the Pacific and settled there as well all the way to California. In fact, American Indians told that Black men with curly hair made trips from California's shores to the pacific on missions of trade. Seafarers crossing the Pacific back and forth to California are much older than the actual divulgence by Spanish explorers.

On the other hand, West Africa trade with the Americas before Columbus and way back to proto-historic times (30,000 BC-10,000 BC) is one of the most important chapters in ancient African history. Yet this era, which began about thirty thousand years ago and perhaps earlier (see *Gladwin Thesis* by C. S. Gladwin, Mc Graw Hill Books), had not been part of the history of Blacks in Americas later on in history, particularly during the early bronze age.

However, during the latter part of the bronze age, particularly between 1500 BC and 1000 BC, when the Olmec civilization began to bloom and flourish, new conditions in the Mediterranean made it more difficult for West Africans to trade by sea with the region, although their land trade across the Sahara was flourishing by then, and others were trying to gain control of the sea routes and the trading ports of the region. Conflict in the region may have pushed the West Africans to strengthen their transatlantic trade with the Americas and to explore and settle there.

BLACK GOD WHITEWASHED IN RECENT HISTORY

Black Madonna of Europe. As the worship of Isis was suppressed, the Virgin Mary was elevated into European Christendom. The African Isis was worshipped under the name of the Virgin Mary." Notice in the above pictures how Black Madonna has been whitewashed as Mary and child.

BLACK GOD WHITEWASHED IN RECENT HISTORY

BLACK GOD WHITEWASHED IN RECENT YEARS

In a two-volume work titled *A Book of the Beginnings*, originally published in 1881, author Gerald Massey recorded it is not necessary to show that first colonizers of India were Black, but it is certain that the Black Buddha of India was imaged in the Africoid type. In the Black (African) god, whether called Buddha or Sut-Nahs, we have a datum. They carry in their color the proof of their origin.

BLACK GODS WHITE WASHED IN RECENT HISTORY

written by: Tracy

The Brahma Samhita is a Sanskrit Pancaratra text composed of verses of prayer spoken by Brahma glorifying the supreme Lord Krishna or Govinda at the beginning of creation. The lyrics, chapter 5, "The primeval Lord, who plays on his transcendental flute. His eyes are like lotus flowers, he is decorated with peacock plumes and his bodily color resembles the color of a fresh Black cloud, although his bodily features are more beautiful of Cupids"

Chapter verse 1,2 reads, "The Lord was dressed in yellow garments and had a blackish complexion." The Sanskrit word krishna has the literal meaning "black," "dark," or "dark blue." Krishna is also called Sama the Blackish.

BLACK JEAN BAPTISTE POINT DU SABLE

On August 28, 1818, Jean Baptiste was regarded as the first permanent resident of what became Chicago, Illinois. Little is known of his life prior to the 1770s. In 1779, he was living on the site of present-day Michigan City, Indiana. Before moving to settle at the mouth of the Chicago River, he is the first recorded living in Chicago in early 1790, having apparently established there some time earlier. He sold his property in Chicago in 1800 and moved to Saint Charles, Missouri, where he died on August 28, 1818, born unknown from Haiti.

BLACK HUMANS ARE MELANIN-DOMINANT PEOPLE

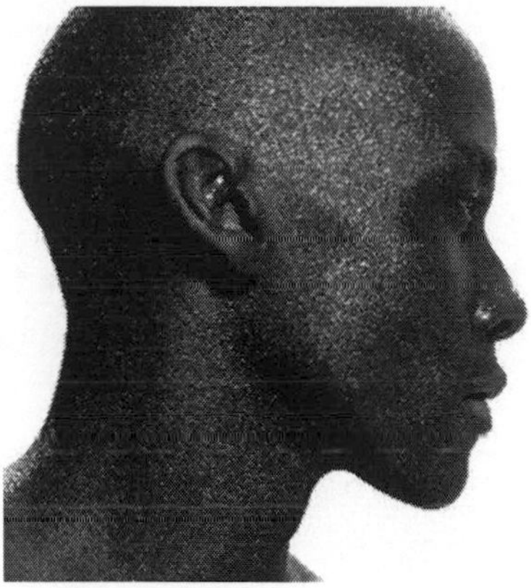

So many Black people are unaware melanin control and manipulate their bodies. The real key to controlling Black people is by reducing their blackness (melanin usage and knowledge). This will reduce their very ability to be black, which will directly affect their ability to be human and seek what is humanly theirs. The fact of the matter is Black people have the highest amount of biochemical pigmentation called melanin. Melanin is a civilized chemical, reproduces itself, and a free radical protector. It can be transformed in the blood, concentrates in nerve and brain information, neutralizes, oxidizes (break down) convert substances, produces (build) another substance and unchanged by radiation or high temperatures. Melanin is inside and outside the body. The more melanin a people have, the more enlightened and refined they are.

The simplest way to explain color black in human is to say you are the only natural human. Examples, watered-down liquor is weaker, and add cream to coffee, then it is weaker. The blacker you are, the much better you are doing anything.

The secret is you have a greater concentration of melanin in the body. Every people of color on earth have been stripped of their true identity in a white-people-controlled power structure. White people destroyed and explained away evidence over three hundred thousand years of civilization built by Black Africans then claim all history was White people's, but White people have only 1,800 years of civilized history.

BLACK PEOPLE YOU NEED TO KNOW

Melanin serves Black people's physical, mental, emotional, and spiritual life. The scientific evidence of melanin threatens the concept of White supremacy. After considering melanin to be a "waste" product of body metabolism, which "served no useful function," Western (White Americans) scientists have now discovered that melanin is the chemical key to life. All studies of facts about melanin suggest that after four hundred years of attempting to make Black people inferior, "Western science is facing the sobering reality that, by its own self-defined standards, Black people are probably superior to Whites in both intellectual potential and physical" (*Sepia* magazine interview). The central role melanin plays in the Black people's body has been "suppressed to maintain the mythological inferiority of Blacks . . . and the defensive clinging to whiteness as some token of superiority" (Dr. Richard King). The "superiority complex" in White people is a defense mechanism and covering their deepest inferiority, which they projected on to people of color. Psychologists say insistent denial means reality in the opposite way. If Whites really believed that white skin is "superior," why is "tanning" in white culture despite its known health risks (thousands die annually from skin cancer), also curling and perming lifeless, straight hair and lip injections for a fuller look and padding their butt for a bigger booty? It is the white female who tells you that her ideal mate is "tall, dark, and handsome"; "dark," indeed, refers to melanin.

SCIENCE CONTENT

content of the physical, spiritual and melanin

BLACK POWER

TYROSINE CHEMICAL STRUCTURE

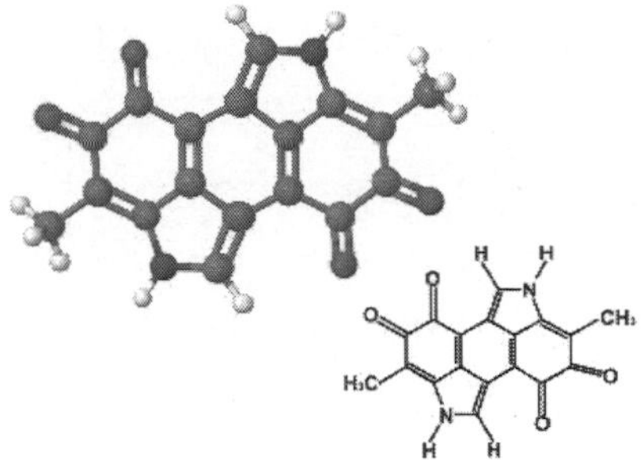

The Amino Acid Called Tyrosine

Many years ago, I was studying biochemistry. Professor MD of chemistry, my instructor, told me that tyrosine was a nonessential amino acid, then he said it was responsible for the pigmentation of the skin, hair, and eyes. I did research on tyrosine and found out that we are preoccupied with color of skin, hair, and eyes.

Broaden the understanding as to what constitute pieces of your body functions; every human body has genes (pieces of DNA in it), in it a need to read the blue print of the pieces of DNA then follow instructions and make proteins. After they are made, the proteins work together and keep your body running. A melanocyte (cell producing and containing melanin) has proteins. These proteins act like workers in an assembly line and carry out steps for making hair, skin, eye colors, and other things like making black people hear, think, taste, and absorb energies better, protect them from damaging effect of sunlight, and slow their aging process. All this started out with a chemical called tyrosine. One changes the tyrosine. Another links these modified tyrosines together making a long chain. The result is melanin. Tyrosine is converted to hormones that have a profound influence on the body's overall condition. Melanin reflects in the way Black people walk, think, and talk. The more concentrated melanin is in the body, the blacker, stronger, and much more intelligent the body is. Melanin conducts and transports information in the body, I concluded in my research when I found the organization the Black National Defense Committee. I designed a rubber stamp of molecular structure of tyrosine and called it the Stamp of Black Power as the Black National Defense Committee seal.

BLACK QUEEN CHARLOTTE SOPHIA OF ENGLAND

Picture from pexel.com

About 250 years ago, even before there was USA, King George III, Britain's most famous king, as far as Americans are concerned, married a Black woman in Saint James Palace.

HITLER FAMILY

White Hitler's family had Black blood reported *New York Times* July 1, 1940. The Huns (Attila the Hun) included Black Mongolians who mixed heavily with the Aryan Germans.

Suzar quote "blackout through whitewash"

BLACK NORWAY KING

Halfdan the Black, who was an Africoid, was the first king to unite Norway.

BLACK VIKINGS

suzar quote

When the British Isles were invaded by the Vikings, some of these Norse raiders were Africoids. In fact, different varieties of Viking Africans lived in Scandinavia during the Middle Ages and are frequently mentioned in Viking sagas.

THERE WERE BLACK HUNS

The dictionary describes the Huns as "a fierce barbaric race of Asiatic nomads who, led by Attila, ravaged Europe in the fourth and fifth centuries AD." Gothic writer Jordanne's description of their infamous leader Attila the Hun was "having a flat nose and swarthy complexion." He described the types of Huns he had seen as "of dark complexion, almost black . . . broad shoulder, flat nose, and small eyes.

TRUE, BEETHOVEN IS BLACK, SO ARE SIX US PRESIDENTS

pexel.com

Beethoven is a dark Moorish mulatto called the Black Spaniard. His teacher, the immortal Joseph Hayden, was also a mulatto! (*Khamit-kush: What They Never Told You in History Class*) In *Five Negro Presidents*, J. A. Rogers documents the mulatto identity of five American presidents (Thomas Jefferson, Alexander Hamilton, Warren Harding, Andrew Jackson, and Abraham Lincoln; Barack Obama is sixth).

AFRICA ADVANCE KNOWLEDGE OF CELESTIAL

Wise men of Africa Dogon tribe baffle scientists with their accurate, advanced technical knowledge of celestials, such as the invisible white dwarf star Sirius B, only recently discovered by science. Africans even accurately told the composition of the moon in 1946, decades before the first moon landing! (Marcel Griaule conversations with Ogotemmeli)

THE INTELLIGENCE OF BLACKS IN MODERN TIMES

Modern inventions of Blacks are many, including automatic transmission, air conditioning, multiple-stage rocket turbine engine, toilet, and traffic lights. Numerous Blacks contribute to the development of microcomputers and the atom bomb. Details; Van Sertima "Blacks in science for quick review",; Ersky Freeman; "1001 Black Inventions supplement."

THE ORIGINAL CHRISTIANS WERE THE ESSENES

Jesus (real name Yehoshua) was an Essene. The earliest image of Jesus, his mother and disciples, and other biblical characters were first seen in the catacombs of Rome, where these early Christians (Essenes) buried their dead. They are portrayed Black. These Essenes, in fact, were the "early Christians" who were brutally persecuted by the White Romans and often fed to the lions for entertainment!

THE ORIGINAL CHRISTIAN CHURCH

The original Christian church was also African (Ethiopian). Its original African founders and early saints were often willingly suffered death rather than renounce their religion, when this church was taken by force, without legal rights, by the Whites who replaced it with their counterfeit Roman Catholic Church.

KNOWLEDGE CONCEALED BY WHITES

The Dead Sea Scrolls exposes knowledge concealed by White Christianity. They prove that Christianity was an outgrowth of Essenism. In the Dead Sea Scrolls and the life of the ancient Essenes, Dr. R. Bernard writes, "These scrolls reveal knowledge hidden from the world ever since the Alexandrian library were burnt by the Roman churchmen in order to purposely destroy it, because they consider it dangerous to the existence and survival of the new religion (False Christianity) which they elaborated by alteration of the original doctrines taught by the Essenes centuries previously."

JESUS YEARS CONCEALED BY ROMANS

The "lost" years of Jesus were deliberately concealed by Roman churchmen, along with most of the deeper, esoteric (understood by or meant for a select few) teaching of original Christianity, which included reincarnation and karma. Fragments of these teachings remain in the Bible, for example, John the Baptist was the reincarnation of the prophet Elijah the prophet (Matthew 11:11-14, Malachi 4:5). Reincarnation and karma explain much of the seeming unbalances in the world. Other biblical reference for both: Job 1:21; John 9:2; Mark 8:27, 28; Revelation 13:10; Obadiah 1:15. A book providing most of the biblical references is *Edgar Cayce on Reincarnation* (also see Montgomery: *A World Beyond*). There is evidence that during the "lost" years of Christ, he traveled/studied in Egypt and India, where early Christians went for advance education. For light on Jesus hidden years/teachings; Levi. "The Aquarian Gospel of Jesus the Christ."

THE WORD "CHRIST"

The word Christ is from Krishna (Christna). Krishna was a great avatar (savior) in India three thousand years before Jesus. The name of the historical man was Yehoshua (or Jeshua), not Jesus.

RELIGION CONTENT

THE ORIGINAL NAME FOR JESUS

Jesus the Panther? An original name for Jesus was Jehoshua Ben Pandira, which means "Jesus, Son of the Panther." (Blavatsky: *The Secret Doctrine*) Even the Bible refers to him as the lion of the tribe of Juda. (Revelation 5:5) "Jesus, in fact, was a Black nationalist freedom fighter . . . whose goals were to free the Black people of that day from the oppressive . . . White Roman power structure and to build a Black nation" (.

Schoenfield reports in *The Passover Plot,* p. 194, "Galilee, where Jesus had lived . . . which was the home of the Jewish resistance movement, suffered particularly. The Romans never cease night and day to devastate . . . pillage [and kill]."

In *The Black Messiah*, p. 91, Rev. A. B. Cleage Jr. writes that Jesus was a revolutionary who was leading a [Black] nation into conflict against an [white] oppressor . . . It was necessary that he be crucified because he taught revolution." Jesus states, "I have not come to send peace, but a sword."

OTHERS CRUCIFIED

The world has had sixteen crucified saviors, all with virgin births, accompanied by stars and other wonders. These saviors *predated* Jesus (Jeshua) by thousands of years! Read *The World's Sixteen Crucified Saviors* by Kersey Graves.

CHRISTIANITY BEFORE YESHUA

Christianity existed long before Christ, well documented in John Jackson's *Christianity before Christ*. Many Bible stories, traditions, special words were copied from Egypt (Kemet) of Africa, Sumer, India, and other cultures. Example, The word "hell" (in dictionary) is from *hel*, the underworld of the Norse myth. The word "Amen" is from Kemet of Africa. The word *El* or *Al* (in Micheal, Gabriel, Daniel, Elohim) was the Canaanite name for "God." Egyptians and Canaanite got their religious words from Kemet of Africa, from which *Amen* or *Amun* is the spiritual name of the "sunset." The original cross used by the early Christians was the Egyptian ANKH, a loop cross which symbolizes everlasting life. The White man's false replacement—the crucifix, cross—is a symbol of death.

THE BLACK MADONNA IS A COPY OF ISIS

The Christian Madonna statue (Mother Mary and Son Jesus) is copied from the Egyptian Madonna, worshipped in Egypt and Rome. Black Isis and her son Horus were the models for the worship of the *Madonna and Christ.* Right now, millions of Whites worship the Black Madonna and Christ found in Europe's most venerated shrines (formerly the site of temples of Isis) with titles such as "Our Lady." The word "Madonna" itself is from *mater donna,* a title used for Isis. Isis existed thousands of years before Mary and Christ (the Black Madonna).

THE RENAISSANCE WAS THE "WHITE ASSISTANCE" OF THE EUROPEANS TO MASSIVELY WHITEWASH AFRICAN HISTORY

It's an ironic shame that such deceptive words or actions to cover up should take place at this time since it was the Africans (Moors) who sparked the Renaissance in the first place! The Catholic Church, using Michelangelo, Leonardo da Vinci, and other artists, was the chief culprit! An overview of the profoundly-wicked history of the Catholic Church and its popes is presented in *Deceptions and Myths of the Bible* by Lloyd Graham. The surviving art that escaped deceptive words or actions to cover up often portrays rulers, famous figures, and armies of knights as dark as they can be. A good source of such art are "icon" art books like Russian icons available at most art museums. Also, at the library, you may find art books on these periods, and if you look carefully through them, you will usually find one or two stray pieces of Black evidence that escaped Renaissance's deceptive words or actions to cover up.

WHITES HAVE DONE A PHENOMENAL JOB OF STEALING, FALSIFYING HISTORY

Napoleon was speaking truth when he said, "History is a lie agreed upon." And Hitler said, "The bigger the lie, the more people will believe it." History is "his" story or the White man's story (his lie), but the truth is coming to light, and the great White lies and deceptions are being exposed as the minds and hearts of humanity reawaken in the increasing light of a new dawn.

BLACK PEOPLE IN AMERICA THOUSANDS OF YEARS BEFORE WHITE PEOPLE

Black people were the first people to enter the Americas, and they laid the foundation of Mesoamerican civilization. When the Mayans voyaged across the Atlantic to the Americas, the Black Olmecs civilization was already deeply rooted in America. The Mayans were the successor of the Olmecs. They were, therefore, not the first to occupy the Yucatan and gulf region of Mexico. Harold Sterling Gladwin, in his book *Men Out of Asia*, he classified four distinct migrants that made use of the Bering Isthmus (Baringa or Bering Strait) to cross over to America. They were the Australoid (who were akin to the Australian aborigines), the Asiatic Negroid (Black Asian), the Algonquins, and the Eskimos. Thus, to Gladwin, Blacks were the first inhabitants of Americas. However, mention must be made of the Dwarf or Pygmies. They were the first humans, and their remains have been found all over the world, including North and South America.

CHIAPAS IN MEXICO IS ONE OF THE ARE MANY ANCIENT BLACK AFRICAN-BUILT CITIES IN THE AMERICAS

Numerous sculpture heads have been discovered throughout Mexico that show the earliest people here during the preclassic period were Africans.

The major African community in Chiapas was located at Chiapa De Corzo, situated on the lowland trench of the Grijalva River. Here, as early as 1400 BC, we find the earliest African American community in Mexico. The people of Chiapas made fine sculptures that show the population was predominately Africans until the late preclassic period. They made their first pyramid in 550 BC.

DESCENDANTS OF PRE-COLUMBIAN BLACKS IN THE UNITED STATES, CENTRAL AMERICA, AND SOUTH AMERICA AND THE FIGHT FOR THE RETURN OF THEIR STOLEN OCCUPIED LANDS

In the midst of the reparations debate, the issue of returning the lands of these Blacks, whose ancestors were here in the United States and Americas before Columbus, has already been done with one Black Indian nation of the Louisiana Territory.

The experience of the Washitaw Nation (or Ouchita Nation) of Southern United States is another piece of solid evidence of pre-Columbian African presence and settlement in the Americas, specifically in the United States. According to an article carried in the magazine. "The freedom press newsletter", Spring 1996, reprinted "from Earth Ways", The Newsletter of the Sojourner Truth Farn School (August, 1995), the Washitaw were (and still are) a nation of Africans who existed in the Southern United States and Mississippi Valley region long before the sixteenth-century Europeans came and even before there were Native Americans on the lands the Washitaw once occupied and still occupy today.

According to the article, the Washitaw nation governed 3 million acres of land in Louisiana, Arkansas, Oklahoma, Texas, and Mississippi. They were shipbuilders (similar to the Garifuna of the Caribbean, who are also of pre-Columbian West African Mandinka Muslim origins, according to Harold Lawrence in *African Presence in Early America*, edited by Ivan Sertima).

What is even more fascinating about this aspect of hidden history of Blacks in America before Columbus is that the Washitaw nation was known and recognized as a separate, independent Black nation by the Spanish and French, who were in Louisiana Territory and Texas areas.

EGYPT IS NOT THE MOTHER OF CIVILIZATION

The most ancient Egyptians were Black Africans. Flinders Petrice begins the history of Egypt with the Bushmen or Black Africans before 8000 BC. Abundant evidence of their presence has been unearthed. The Ethiopians of Africa also claim, states that Egyptians are a colony drawn from Ethiopia, and that Egypt was made out of the mud and slim of Ethiopia. Further, according to the ancient writers, the Egyptians got their laws, their customs, their burial rites, their statutes, and their system of writing from Ethiopia. Egyptians gods were of Ethiopian ancestry and recognized it by the high esteem in which they held the Ethiopians and their annual return to Ethiopia for feasting. Egyptian history and modern excavations support these assertions. Most of the records have been lost, and the little that remain must be pieced together. Right now, as you read this, the Europeans are trying to take Egypt out of Africa. Ethiopians were the founders of Egypt.

EMPEROR OF MALI MANSA MUSA

It has been recorded that Mansa Musa carried a lot of gold on his trip to Mecca in an act of religious devotion. In 1324, he spent extravagantly, which made the price of gold fall for ten years. Manus Musa created the library of Timbuktu, and the original texts in Timbuktu, the work surrounds all area of world information and qualifications (ability to do something well) written during his reign. Mali had four hundred cities, and the Niger Delta was very populated. Mali Timbuktu had 115,000 people living there at that time, which is five times more than (in the Middle Ages) London. Timbuktu, at that time, was in good standing, with a high mental capacity with culture and a beautiful lifestyle. There are old handwritten or printed works that date back to hundreds of years ago in the possession of many old

African homes who have private libraries (shyyyyyy, don't tell the White people). Even Mauritanian cities of Chingeutti and Ouadane have an estimated 3,450 books written by hand. It's possible that there six thousand books still in existence in the city of Walata, which go back to eighth century AD. There are evidence that there eleven thousand books in private library collections in Niger. Prof. Henry Luis Gates said approximately twenty-five thousand university students studied there, and recently, Timbuktu have been defined as the Paris of the medieval world. Timbuktu itself have approximately seventy thousand books in continuance, which is written in different languages: Mande, Suqi, Fulani, Timbuktu, and Sudani. The books include math, medicine, poetry, law, and astronomy. It is known to be the first encyclopedia. The Europeans were still sleeping with their livestock and very uneducated when this scientific world was blooming.

EUROPE IS A BLACK NAME

Europe named after the Black Phoenician Europa, who was kidnapped by Black Zeus.

EVIDENCE OF BLACK AFRICAN CIVILIZATION IN AMERICA

The exceptionally natural capacity of intellect of Black Africans to carve history in stone, showing evidence that Black Africans were the first people in America as early as 100,000 years ago. The Black African gigantic stone heads, terracotta's, stone pyramids and Black female bones, over 300,000 years old is found, not just America, but all over the world. Black African Americans can claim it in the form of direct identity.

Today the receiving containing of the mind of the American people and some parts of the world, rejects what is historical facts of the Black people. Then you are psychologically impaired, it is characterized by persisting learning that which damages your physical, mental, emotional and spiritual life when you believe in something that you don't understand. while some of the American people will not perceived ancient Black history, facts immediately but the series experiencing the mind and the body you will began to see the truth and the minds of the young people will be free when they know their true identity.

When you know the truth about Black history, and you speak the truth, the world will stop and turn its ears to hear you.

FACE OF AFRO-OLMEC CHILD CARVED ONTO THE WAIST BELT OF AN OLMEC BALL PLAYER FOUND IN AMERICA, EVIDENCE THAT AFRICAN PEOPLE WERE ALREADY IN AMERICA FOR THOUSANDS OF YEARS

This stone belt was used by the Olmec ball players to catch the impact of the rubber balls in their ball games. This face is typical Nigritic, including the eyes, which seem to slant, a common racial characteristic in West Africa, the Sahara, and in South Africa among the Kong-San (Bushmen) and other Africans.

FACT: JESUS IS A BLACK MAN

Facts have unholy tendencies to be get the truth, reality, Jesus is a black man. Over time the false images have impregnated the minds of the masses to such a stage that the notion of the Messiah being Black would seem like a disagreeable impossibility. Many people, especially Black people, regard a general understanding that the Messiah and the disciples being Black was an attempt to instill Black pride in the Black people rather than considering if it could be true or not. White American people have brainwashed the general public to such a condition that when you try to tell people the truth, they won't receive it because they have been taught so long to believe in lies.

All the images and paintings that were displayed in churches today are of a guy by the name of Cesare Borgia. In case you never heard of this name before, Cesare Borgia was a homosexual Italian mobster and a captain in the papal military during the 1500s. He was also the son of Pope Alexander VI of Rome. The earliest visual depiction of Jesus is a painting that was found in 1921 on a wall of the baptismal chamber of the house church at Dura Europos, Syria, and dated around AD 235. The painting is called *Healing the Paralytic Man* (Mark 2:1-12), and it described him being short and dark-skinned with a small curly Afro.

According to Eisler reconstruction, the oldest non-biblical description of Jesus reads as follows: "At that time also thee appeared a certain man of magic power . . . if it be meet to call him a man, whom people call a son of God, but his disciples the true prophet . . . He was a man of simple appearance, mature age, Black skinned short growth, three cubits tall. This short, black-skinned, mature, hunchbacked Jesus with a unibrow, short curtly hair, and undeveloped beard bears no resemblance to the Jesus Christ taken for granted today.

White people (Paleolithic, humanoid, hybrid, or andro) have disgraced the very spirit of thousands of years of the hue-man (dark-skinned) religion. The life force receptacle is encrypted in every living hue-man (brown/dark-skinned). It cannot be stolen or changed. It is in hue-man's physical, mental, emotional, and spiritual life. Lies, falsification, and denial will not work.

THE CATHOLIC EVIL DECEIT

The Catholics have convinced practically the whole world that Cesare is the image of Jesus. Though not everyone revered him as a son of God, people were drawn by the elegance and beauty of his image, accepted it and took it to be their son of God. Catholics did this to deceive the world, while People began attributing this guy as the son of God, thus fulfilling Revelation 12:9: "And the great dragon was cast out that old serpent, called the Devil and Satan which deceived the whole world: He was cast out into the earth, and his angels were cast out with him."

So Satan, with the help of the Catholic Church, has deceived people around the world into thinking Cesare Borgia is Jesus Christ. What did Satan say? Isaiah 14:14: "I will ascend above the heights of the clouds; I will be like most high." So through this false image of Jesus, Satan gets the glory as if he was God like he said. Now you see why the Catholic Church took the Apocrypha (group of fourteen books written by King Solomon) out of the Holy Bible. They didn't want to get exposed. Little did they know the real, the true, all-natural human being will come along one day and show Satan (humanoid) for what they really are.

ALL RELIGIONS AROUND THE WORLD, ON EVERY CONTINENT, WERE FOUND BY A BLACK HUMAN BEING

The picture you see above, like so many pictures today, is a White fake Jesus, A white man on a cross, dressed in traditional robe and sometimes barefooted, it is a plain fake. The white man in the picture, the popular image of Jesus Christ and worshipped today by millions of people, is Cesare Borgia. Leonardo da Vinci was employed by Cesare Borgia for about a year to work as an engineer and military architect, and there were rumors that they had a homosexual relationship. Pope Alexander asked the Catholic Church to accept his son's image as that of Jesus Christ. Jesus Christ is Hebrew before he was charged for excommunication, and all Hebrews are black. The above painting of Cesare Borgia was done in the sixteenth century. Cesare Borgia is a white homosexual.

FAKE WHITE JESUS WAS NECESSARY TO RULE THE WORLD

Apollonius, sometimes called Apollonius of Tyana, born and died in first to second century AD, was a Greek philosopher from the town of Tyana, the Roman province of Cappadocia in Anatolia. Being a first-century orator and philosopher around the time of Jesus, he was compared with Jesus of Nazareth by Christians in the fourth century and by other writers in modern times.

There have been many white faces posing today as Jesus, but there is only one Jesus, and he is a Black man (name: Yahusha), hair in dreads, and he is Hebrew. The above picture is a true example of White people identity theft: *blacked out through whitewash.*

THE GENETIC KEY TO HUMANITY: WE ARE NOT THE SAME

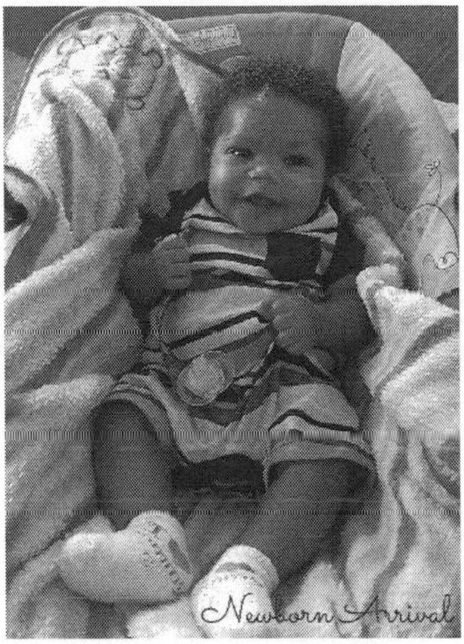

Do not believe in the theory that we are all the same. For those of you who hate who you are and love who you want to be should be informed now that you are the first human (hue-man) to walk this earth, put here by nature—better word, put here by God. The pineal gland is what makes you different. It produces melanin. Melanin is the key to life. The more melanin you have, the more civilized you are. The more melanin you have, the more psychic you are. The more melanin you have, the more information can be stored in the brain. You can see full and complete colors. Other people cannot see full colors like you. You can taste complete flavors of your food. That is why your food is called soul food. You can hear complete sounds. Other people cannot hear complete sounds. They act like they hear, but they can't, and it shows in their untrained dance that they can't hear full sound. That is why Black people's music is called soul music. Melanin has memory. Sometimes you remember how to do things that your ancestors did thousands of years ago. It is in the melanin. Europeans have a convention every two or three years to discuss melanin, all about nothing but melanin. They never invite Black people to that convention. A study was once done to children, between zero to twenty-four months, of all parts of the world. The purpose of the study was to find out if there was a genetic link to people's abilities in nature and the world or universe regarded as an orderly, harmonious system. To the surprise of the European scholars, the African child dominated, in all aspects, his Caucasian counterpart. The following data was obtained:

Babies, being drawn up unto a sitting position, able to prevent the head from falling backward: Black child - 9 hours old; White child - 6 weeks old

With the head held firmly, looking at the face of the examiner: Black child - 2 days old; White child - 8 weeks old

Supporting himself/herself in a sitting position and watching his/her reflexes in the mirror: Black child - 7 weeks old; White child - 20 weeks old

Holding himself/herself upright: Black child - 5 months old; White child - 9 months old

Age at which the child knew his/her own name: Black child - 8 months old; White child - 14 months old

Age at which the child could use three or more words appropriately: Black child - 10 months old; White child - 12 months old

Climbing the steps alone: Black child - 11 months old; White child - 15 months old

Standing against the mirror: Black child - 5 months old; White child - 9 months old

The conclusion from this and other comparative studies of Black and White children in Africa, Europe, and America was that the African is significantly advanced over the White child up to the age of two. After this age, White society steps in, beginning to shape up the Black child's physical, mental, and emotional life, affected by what the parents eat, wear, watch on TV, etc. Then the condition is compounded in White public school system. Common term used is that your child will be dumbed down.

WHY THE BLACK PEOPLE ARE SO IMPORTANT TO THE WORLD

Imagine what goes through the mind of a person who hates who they are and love who they want to be. I'm talking about the melanated people (dark hue/dark-skinned).

Melanin is the key to life. White people hold a convention in Europe periodically, discussing in session all about melanin. They need to know how to use melanin to benefit the White people. Right now, sunglasses have vegetable melanin in them to protect the Paleolithic (paleface) eyes. Many people think that sunglasses is a fashion statement, but little do they know that sunglasses are needed for White people's eyes, but sunglasses have a damaging effect on melanated people's eyes. Pure White people suffer severe burns from the sun, especially when close to the equator. In USA alone, one hundred thousand suffer sunburn and skin cancer and ten thousand die from skin cancer. Right now, the birth rate in some parts of the world among White people is -3 (minus three). Here, in America, fertility banks are being suited because they cannot impregnate the White female. Now the White people want to control the birth rate of the dark hue people here in USA. There are ongoing studies and research on aborted Black babies (fetus), how to use the pineal gland to benefit white people. The known secret is that melanin is scientifically unclassified, only in theory. I have a theory $%#^&*(+ I'm going to live to two hundred years old. Annually, thousands of Black people are being kidnapped for body parts. A healthy Black person could be worth US$1 million on the black market. Read *The Immortal Life of Henrietta Lacks* by Rebecca Skloot. She tells you what can be done with the Black (dark hue/dark-skinned) body.

While you hate who you are and love who you wanna be, the greatest composition of nature today is the black human. Anything existed after the black human is a derivative of living human form.

BLACK AFRICAN HANNIBAL OF CARTHAGE, FATHER OF MILITARY STRATEGY, 247-183 BC

Hannibal had the reputation of being the greatest military leader and strategist of all time. It has been said by many experts that among seven supreme military geniuses of the world, Hannibal ranks as the first in daring. The most audacious of all, most astonishing perhaps, so bold, so sure, so great in everything, Hannibal, at twenty-six years of age, conceived what is hardly conceivable. He executed what one may truly call the impossible. After Carthage, Hannibal's father, gave Hannibal permission to take over the great army, he thanked him and succeeded to the supreme command of the peninsula. He defeated all the tribes until only one remained—the Sagentum, allies of Rome. Hannibal did not hesitate and engaged a bloody battle and defeated them. Hannibal defeated Rome's ablest general and foremost counsellor Fabius the Great. And Hannibal defeated Scipio. In a bloody attack,

Hannibal defeated the great commander and killed Sempronius. He defeated Rome general Flaminius, taking all North Italy.

Hannibal recruited men from the Numidians, Africans, Spaniards, and Gauls, taking measures of one battle success. Rome lost twenty-five thousand men; Hannibal lost fifteen hundred. The deciding battle was when Hannibal killed seventy thousand Roman men, General Emilius, and with him, eighty Roman senators. The above is pictures of Hannibal on a corn; Hannibal issued those corns to his men.

THE HISTORICAL EVILNESS OF HANNAH DUSTON

The name "Redskin" is the name white people use in glorifying the victory of killing Black Indians. The Albano was the first to start scalping; there was a bounty for a scalp of a Black Indian. Historian Prof. Roxanne Dunbar-Ortiz stated that the American settlers were paid bounties for killing Indians, and they gave a name to the mutilated and bloody corpse they left in the wake of their scalp hunts: *Redskins*!

The term "albino" was used to describe what we call the White people, and the Black Indians were called Black Indians

OBSERVING THE STATUE ERECTED IN AMERICA: The inscription underneath tells of her 1697 actions in an Indian raid and how she massacred twelve women and children as they slept. Later she returned for their scalps, having remembered they could fetch a bounty.

Today we have been lied to in history, and in false repeats of the old western movies, "THE INDIANS WERE BLACK."

BLACKNESS: HOW DOES MELANIN CAUSE RACIAL DIFFERENCES

Science shows that Blacks can produce all races, but it is impossible for a brown, yellow, or white race to produce a Black race. A Japanese scientist showed that inside melanocytes (pigment cells) are tiny packets called melanosomes that contain melanin. The four stages in the maturing of these melanosomes count for racial difference. Stage 1: The melanocytes is empty and don't have machinery to make melanin. Stage 2: The melanosome has the machinery to make melanin but is empty of melanin. Stage 3: The machinery is there, and the melanosomes is half full with melanin. Stage 4: The machinery is there, and the melanosome is completely filled with melanin. White people have mainly stages 1 and 2, whereas all people of color have melanin, with Blacks having more of stage 4.

BLACK AFRICAN KING TUTANKHAMUN, ANCIENT EGYPTIAN PHARAOH OF AFRICA

Tutankhamun was only eight or nine when he became ruler of Egypt. Tutankhamun was only king for about ten years. It was estimated that he ruled from 1333 B C to 1324 BC. Tutankhamun married his half sister; his father was Akhenaten. Akhenaten was married to Nefertiti, who bore him six daughters. Akhenaten also had a lesser wife, Kira, who gave birth to Tutankhamun. Tutankhamun married Ankhesenpaaten, one of the daughters of Akhenaten and Nefertiti. About King Tut's death, that he suffered a blow to the back of the head, accidentally or deliberately (murder), or that he broke or fractured his leg, which became infected—an infection that led to his death possibly only days later.

Tutankhamun was born Tutankhamaten. Akhenaten, Tutankhamun's father, wanted Egyptians to worship one god, the sun god Aten, instead of the multitudes of gods they already worshipped, and the main deity Amun. The "Aten" at the end of Tutankhamaten's and Akhenaten's names refers to this (Akhenaten means "servant of the Aten", and Tutankhamaten means "living image of Aten"). Akhenaten's changes weren't too popular, so when Tutankhamaten was in charge, he changed things back to how they were, reopening the various closed temples around the country and changing his name to Tutankhamun. Incidentally, Akhenaten's original name before he started making changes was Amenhotep IV.

KINGDOM OF NRI

The West African region in S Igbo speaking people. The kingdom of Nri was different in the state or government. Having a king, its leader was armed with no military power. The kingdom of Nri was not like any other form of world government. Its leader exercised no military power over his subjects, southwestern Nigeria. . The Igbo history is very old. Their culture spread from Nigeria to northeast and south Africa, giving social, religious, and government, to the world.

Etymology: Chronological account of the birth and development of a particular word, often delineating its spread from one language to another and its evolving changes in form and meaning.

The Igbo language is found in all the different languages around the world. Igbo power of communication in words alone, together with their spiritual level. The intensity created harmony achieved in the power of speaking words. The Igbo language was designed to create to cause and come into being the unitary whole of act or ; enable individual to participate and get special result of one's efforts by matching words with certain action or motion a word conveys. The act or process allows individuals to express themselves without the use of force. The Igbo lifestyle or way of life has been in existence for thousands of years, enabling speech, organizing societies, governments, and communication throughout the world. Think about when contracts and agreements were done simply by a hand shake after words of agreements.

White Europeans invaded Nigeria, force-fed White Christianity, destroying the Igbo way of life, killing about 1.5 million Igbos. Now crime, mistrust, and violence have contaminated the very ground Igbo walk on.

MAAT THE ANCIENT AFRICAN GODDESS OF TRUTH, JUSTICE, AND MORALITY

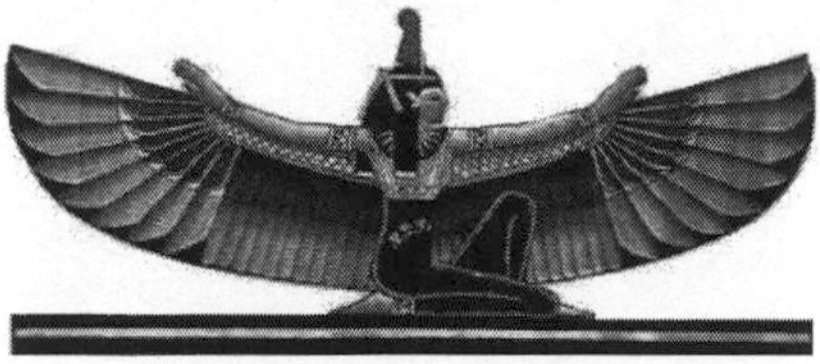

It is deceiving for Egypt of Africa to try and separate the spiritual and moral order from Kemet. Maat is a word of Kemet of Africa, represented by a female figure, meaning spiritual and moral order, everywhere at the same time throughout the universe. The daughter of the Kemet sun deity Ra and wife of the moon god Thoth, she decided whether a person would successfully reach the afterlife. Maat would put her feather on the scale and the person's heart on the other side. If the heart is heavier than the feather, that person cannot see afterlife. By weighing their soul against her feather of truth was the personification of the cosmic order and a representation of the stability of the universe. Christians, Muslims, and other religious faiths put wings on their angels, imitating Maat. One would wear a feather in his hair, connection to truth, justice, and moral order of Maat. Kemet civilization existed thousands of years before Egypt in East Africa. Egypt is an expression of Kemet consciousness. She got math, trigonometry, geometry, algebra, and science from Kemet. Egypt was able to share it with Europe, thereby Europe assuming ancient civilization began with Egypt. You will find the bird symbol all over the world, example, the United States' eagle.

MANSA MUSA: AFRICAN WORLD'S RICHEST MAN

Mansa Musa named the richest man in history that outranked the Rothchild family of $350 billion and John D. Rockefeller of $340 billion per *New York Daily* news.

Musa, "emperor," of the wealthy West African Mali Empire, was born in 1280 and died in 1337. At time of Musa's rise to the throne, the Malian Empire consisted of territory formerly belongs to the Ghana Empire in present-day Southern Mauritania and in Melle and the immediate surrounding area.

It was said that when Musa travelled, he would upset the economy of other countries. It took Egypt of Africa ten years to recover from Musa's visit to Mecca. Musa's richness consisted of a stunning $400 billion.

BLACK AFRICA MAU MAU AND KENYA

Kenya was invaded by the White Europeans under the authority of the British Empire. The Whites were given land by the British to establish their homes and farms. The land were taken from the Black African Kenyans, and they were forced to live landless and homeless. The Kenyans were called lazy because they refused to work for the Whites. They were unemployed and lived in makeshift shacks as peasants. The Black Kenyans began to take steps and mounted an uprising.

It began as the peasant revolt. The organized movement contacted the homeless, hungry, unemployed, prostitutes, and criminals and had them take an oath to secrecy, joining a movement of freedom. The oath taker went from place to place, talking to the peasants, explaining what their problem was, that their land and homes had been stolen away and given to the white settlers. The British setup an all-White government with the intent to steal and control the populace that were beginning to suffer homeless, starvation, and sickness. It was the major object of the British to deny legitimacy or respectability to the Kenyan people. The oath taken spread like wildfire throughout the country.

After reaching one hundred thousand oath-takers, some of the members were selected to take a stronger oath, which prepared them to commit to guerilla activities. They came down from the mountain, burning and destroying the crops of the White settlers and taking their livestock for food. They also took any guns and clothes. The Whites began to pack up and move out of Kenya. The British Royal Army came in to establish security and order, killing thousands of the guerillas. The guerillas were steadfast until the government began to talk about power transfer.

The Black Kenya people started taking steps to chart out their own government. They organized the Kenya African National Union (KANU), KADU, and other groups to represent the people who had no voice. They established parliament of the lawmaking body then allowed Kenyatta to be the president. It was not easy to reach all the people's needs at the beginning, but in time, it seemed to workout. The biggest problem was distributing land back to the people; the guerillas felt left out at the beginning. The Mau Mau revolt brought about great change, giving the people independence and the freedom of self-determination.

THE METROPOLIS AREAS OF ANCIENT BLACK AFRICA

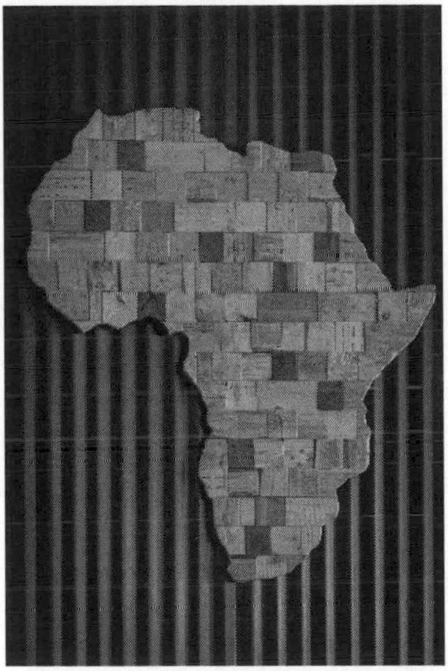

Something amazing is being discovered about Africa. It is the remains of huge metropolis areas that measures in 10,000 square miles and appears to have been constructed 160,000-200,000 years ago. This late discovery was done by Google satellite recently. There are 100,000 of these metropolis (cities) throughout Africa. Africa is bigger than USA, China, India, and all of Europe.

MITOCHONDRIA EVE

When the original analysis of the DNA in the mitochondria of modern humans was carried out, the result suggested that all modern people shared the DNA of a single individual female who lived three hundred thousand years ago. This female was named Eve. Eve's bones were found in Africa. She is a Black woman. The Black woman, in the minds of people with a higher level of consciousness, is put here by the supernatural spiritual force because she gave life to every race of people on earth.

MVLEY ARSHEID ZERIFF: PRINCE OF TAFFELETA AND BLACK AFRICAN EMPEROR OF MOROCCO

His mother was an unmixed Black slave, and he had tens of thousands of White slaves. His picture was painted in 1670. Africa treated their White slaves good, the meanest Christian slave on becoming a Mohammedan was freed, and he and his descendants were eligible to the highest office in the country .

For centuries also and well into 1857, the Black Arabs and Black Africans had been raiding what is now Russia for White slaves.

Mvley Arsheid Zeriff's picture was on the market for sale at 9,999,999 euros. Like Blacks around the world, they are history.

(RELIGOUS CONTENT)

KNOW THE MYTH OF EASTER

Professor Cusack has his brain printed all over this European myth of Easter, supposing, commemorating today the resurrection of Jesus from the dead, written in the New Testament as having occurred on the third day after his burial following his crucifixion by the Romans at Calvary in AD 30. It is interesting to know that Easter actually began as a pagan festival. The pagans would celebrate the beginning of spring. They got more sunshine, more light, more heat, and a beginning of new life in this season of the year. The resurrection of Jesus, by a supernatural force as a good Zombie. Centuries after Jesus's life, Easter is attached to the old pagan festival.

No one knows when the word "Easter" came about. An English monk, saint, and historian wrote the earliest history of England in the eighth century. The word was derived from "Eostre" or "Eostrae," the Anglo-Saxon goddess of spring and fertility.

The Easter bunny first arrived in America in the 1700s with the German immigrants who settled in Pennsylvania and transported their tradition of egg-laying rabbit called Osterhase or Oschter Haws. Their children believed in this myth and made nests in which this creature, the rabbit, could lay its colorful eggs.

Dr. Ray Higgins said it best, "To believe in something you don't understand you suffer." Listen to Steve Wonder.

NAPPY, KINKY HAIR IS DIVINE

Suzar writes about the ancient times in *Blacked Out through Whitewash*. Christ was call the "lamb" of God, with kinky hair comparable to a lamb's wool, feet the color of burned brass (Revelation 1:14, 15), and a likeness resembling a sardine stone, which is commonly a brownish stone (Revelation 4:3). Think about this: How many white American Christians will remain White Christians if they knew Christ was truly a nappy, kinky-haired Black man? The part of the Bible that tells you who Christ really is somehow get explained away to maintain the White inferior race. Like Christ and all the founders of religions, God himself has kinky, nappy hair (God created human in his image; black humans are the first to walk this earth).

The power that causes all galaxies to spiral and planets and atoms to spin, that causes the double helix spiral of the DNA molecules, the same spiraling power causes spiraling hair, otherwise known as nappy kinky, curly, frizzy, wavy, wooly hair. The world spins; spiral and spiritual have common roots. The supreme power spins, spiral; it is spiritual; it moves or spirals the universe, dances in spiral rotation; everything in it reflects the spiraling, spiritual essence out of which it is made!

Hair is really an antenna that receives and transmits energy. Take an ordinary hair comb and comb it through your hair, then wave the comb over a piece of paper. It will, by use of energy from the comb, pick up the paper. Nappy, kinky, and dreadlocks are qualities of Black people that transmit divine energy and inspiration spiritually. Have you heard of the story of Samson? Israelites discovered that his strength was in his long hair, then they cut off his hair and was able to defeat him.

Black people are awakening to true self-knowledge and self-acceptance. ; Nappy hair as good and straight hair as bad.

THE YOUNG KING TUTANKHAMEN

The workmanship of the finest funerary mask ever found in the world is of the highest order. Compared with the face of the mummy and especially sculptured for the king, it appears to be an exact likeness of the young supreme Black ruler. It was made of beaten gold inlaid with semiprecious stones and glass paste. Black Africa had mastered metallic and stone art thousands of years before European civilization.

RICH AND POWER OF TIMBUKTU GAVE THE WORLD THE KEY TO INDUSTRY

Founded in ancient times, in AD 1490, this southern city of Sudan is considered by scholars as one of the world's greatest classics. Africans have a rich folklore of proverbs, and such tales as the uncle Remus story have out of folklore. But probably the most lasting important discoveries of ancient Africa was the smelting of iron, which Africa taught the world. It seems likely that when the European was still satisfied with chipped stone tools, the Africans had invented and adopted the art of smelting iron. Consider for a moment what this meant for the advance of the human race. As long as the hammer, knife, saw drill, spade, and hoe had to be chipped out of stone or had to be made of shell or hard wood, effective industry or work was not impossible but difficult. A great progress was made when copper was found in large nuggets and was hammered out into tools and later on shaped by smelting and when bronze was introduced. But the true advancement of industrial life did not begin until hard iron was discovered. It seems unlikely today that the people who made the marvelous discovery of introducing ore by smelting were Black Africans. Neither ancient Europe nor Western Asia nor ancient China knew iron, and everything points to its introduction to Africa.

SANTA CLAUS IS A BLACK MAN

Saint Nicholas was a Christian bishop of Myra who gave to the poor and sick. That is the reason for Santa Claus today. Black Saint Nicholas was born during the third century in the village of Patara, in what is now the southern coast of Turkey. He was of a very wealthy ethnic Black Anatolians of the Roman Empire. He was one of those ancient Black Moors of Europe. Nicholas's wealthy parents died when he was still young. Being a devout Christian, he followed the words of Jesus to use his whole inheritance to assist the needy, the sick, and the suffering. He was made the bishop of Myra while still a young man. Today you can see White Santa Claus perpetuating what the Black Saint Nicholas did hundreds of years ago. Saint Nicholas died on December 6, AD 343, in Myra and was buried in his cathedral church.

The White image of Saint Nicholas is a true example of deceptive practices or actions to cover up historical facts that Saint Nicholas was Black, not White. Today he is passed off as a White Santa Claus.

SLAVERY AMONG THE ANCIENTS

These White girls who were sold in slavery markets of Greece and Rome came sometimes from even royal families. Such were usually captives. Horace, Roman poet, 65-8 BC, mentioned three of this kind. He says Briseis, though a slave, had power to move Achilles's heart with her white beauty. In general, Whites were sold as slaves in Sallee, Morocco, thousands of years before White people started American slavery of Black people.

TIMBUKTU IN MALI

Timbuktu (or Timbuctoo) is one of the cities destroyed by the White Europeans. In the fourteenth century, Timbuktu was five times bigger than London of England and was the richest city in the world. People there are Africans who, right now, stand on the grounds of Timbuktu, Mali, and not aware of this fact. Now Timbuktu is estimated to be 256 times smaller than London and have no evidence of a modern city. The number of people living in Timbuktu today is one half less than the number people who lived in it five hundred years ago. In the fourteenth century, the three wealthiest places on earth were China, Iran, and Mali Empire in West Africa. Among these three places, Mali Empire was the only one still independent and successful. China and the Middle East were defeated by Genghis Khan's troops and were severely damaged and looted. Mansa Musa was the richest in the history or in the world in Mali. He was also the emperor of the fourteenth-century Mali Empire. The Mali Empire is present-day Mali, Senegal, Gambia, and Guinea. When Mansa Musa died, his net worth was US$400 billion, and he still remains the richest man in history, in the world.

THE AFRICAN CITIES THAT WERE DESTROYED BY THE EUROPEAN

In south of the Sahara Desert, there are no buildings, arranged structures, or monuments, and the White Europeans are responsible for this. Europeans destroyed most of them, leaving only skeletons, but there are written accounts by explorers who came to scrutinize or examine prior to the cities destruction. This is always a concern for people who travel regularly or frequently to countries all over the world and who visited places in Africa. They are wondering why there aren't much historical statues or buildings. Many cities in Africa were deserted and in disrepair when diseases such as small pox, syphilis, influenzas, and other diseases brought by the Europeans began to spread and killed the Africans. Those cities were made to become permanently abandoned. Although a considerable amount of the history of Africa is still actualized. Not visible existing as potential. The degree the Europeans destruction are deeply buried and or covered up. People are beginning to find the truth, facts. My intention is to put light on some of it.

THE BLACK IGBO LANGUAGE GAVE BIRTH TO ALL LANGUAGES

The language of the Igbo people is the leading, most important, and well-known ethnic group language of all Africa, in the South Eastern Nigeria of Africa. The Igbo language is an action-based language. A spiritual energy always precedes action. One may call the Igbo language was designed to cause to come into a system of communication that enables individual to participate knowledge to matching words with certain actions. This allows individuals to express themselves without use of force. The Igbo population spread west to east and north to south of Africa. The Igbo government ruled with no police or military force. The language of communication today came from the Igbo many thousands of years ago. Their contract agreement was bonded with a handshake.

THE CAPITAL OF KAMEN-BORNO AS NGAZARGAMU

The origin of Kanem-Borno is unclear now that the White Europeans used deceptive words or actions to cover up the history of the largest city in the world in AD 1658. The city began developing over a thousand years before the White people collected bits and pieces that suggested the city started sometime AD 700. Their first historical source showed that theory. How much did the Europeans steal or destroy is unknown. The nomadic Tebu-speaking Kanembu were forced southwest toward the rich lands around the Lake Chad under political pressure.

In eleventh century, the Zaghawa clans were driven out the Humal Ibn Salamna and founded the kingdom of Kanem and established the capital at Njimi. There, the Saifwa Dynasty was established, and they ruled for 771 years. By White people's standards, it is the longest known dynasty rule in history.

HENRI CHRISTOPHE (1767—1820) FIRST EUROPE-RECOGNIZED HAITIAN KING

King Henri Christophe, of Igbo ancestry, reigned after the Haitian Revolution (1791-1804) that ended French slavery and colonial rule on that Caribbean island. The loss of the island was a great blow to the great French general Napoleon. He was unable to raise money to support his army, and hence, he had to sell Louisiana to the USA for ½$3.50 an acre. Louisiana, at that time, was one third of the area of the USA.

THE FIRST HUMAN TO WALK THIS EARTH

The first human to walk this earth was a Black female, originated in Africa. Her reproduction was asexual (impregnated without the sperm of a male). This is before her xx chromosomes split, yielding to XY, creating a different type of female. Today we call that other type of female a male. The Black female's body is a temple, and in her virginal is heaven. This makes the Black woman mother of the universe. The higher Black African culture civilization worshipped the Black female as the angel. Her wisdom was very important to the order by which Black human conducted their life. The order has been written by the female Maat. *The Black female is the mother of every human on earth.*

THE FIRST PERSON TO WALK THIS EARTH

Archaeologists and anthropologists from all over the world were unable to arrive with the same data on how old the Black female bones were that was discovered in Black Africa. Some scientists say the bones were three hundred thousand years old, and some say the bones were 1.5 million years old. It is estimated that the Black female existed on earth first, and man came later. In this computer space-age world we live in today, Black (dark hue/dark-skinned/color people) and White people have a problem accepting the above scientific facts. It makes everything you have been learning a lie, untrue, pure bullshit, and just gospel. Have you ever been driving or riding in a car and you feel it didn't run? Right, you stop the car, get out, walk around it, and look for an explanation. The point is you have to step out of your circle of persistent learning and look into the circle, then entertain truths through the mist untold centuries (thousands of years) of available facts these things will come to you as if by a miracle. There were no ancient White Hebrews. Jesus was not born in a barn in Bethlehem, in a manger, and kings and rich men didn't travel 12,000 miles on a camel's back in three days to visit the White baby Jesus. There are no records of Moses in Egypt. Adam and Eve story is a lie. Then you begin to see why the car is not running or riding properly. Think about this: An Black African female came from her grave and gave you a message, but you can't accept it is characterized by persistent learning, something that hinders your physical, mental, emotional, and spiritual being. Then you shall suffer. If you believe Noah's ark being 510 feet long, 85 feet wide, and 51 feet high and that you can get every different species around the world into the ark, don't consider how long it will take, then you are psychologically impaired. Study Dr. Ray Higgins's *Why They Gave Us Christmas*. Remember this: The white people who wrote this bullshit just discovered the earth was round in the AD 1500s. *The Black African lady's bones are physical evidence that she is the first human to walk this earth. She is the mother of every human on earth.*

THE GODDESS ISIS, ALSO CALLED THE QUEEN OF HEAVEN, SUCKING IS HER SON HORUS

Mary and child

Isis and child

In church and school today, you will find the name Mary sometimes relate to the Mother of God. What people don't know is that Mary is a template of Isis, so are many others. You can find information about

Isis and many other gorgeous images of tremendous female figures who were associated to Mary. Mary absorbed Isis's sky goddess characteristics in the European's imagination. Isis is a very old goddess figure. At the time Rome was a great power, Isis of Africa predated Mary thousands of years. That is saying something. She was first a local goddess of North Egypt of Africa, worshipped some time before 3100 B.C. Over time, Isis's popularity increased. Isis was identified with the sky and sun. She was said to be the daughter of the sky goddess. Isis was the wife of Osiris, who died and was reborn and became god of the afterlife. Goddess Isis was often depicted with her child sitting in her lap, mother, queen of heaven, and often as a protector. By the second century AD, she had absorbed the traits of many goddesses like Mary, and now Isis's worship was so common throughout the world. She is known in ten thousand names. Theotokos: How the mother goddess became mother of God 431 A.D., that is the year the Church fathers met in modern day Turkey and officially declared Mary is Theotokos, literately, in Greek, Mary was the one who gave birth to God. More commonly, her title is the mother of God. It was a political step, just another of the thousands imitating Isis.

THE KNOWN PICTURE OF TIMBUKTU OF AFRICA

THE PICTURE YOU SEE IS A FAKE JESUS

The popular image of Jesus Christ worshipped today is based on the paintings that of Cesare Borgia (1475/76-1507). The portrait on the left is said to have been made by Altobello Melone and is considered by tradition to be that of Cesare Borgia.

Leonardo da Vinci was employed by Cesare Borgia to work as an engineer and military architect, and there were rumors that they had a homosexual relationship. Cesare's father, Cardinal Rodrigo de Lanzel y Borgia, who later became Pope Alexander VI, schemed to have the Catholic Church accept his son's image as that of Jesus Christ.

The metamorphosis of Jesus Christ from Black to White started not long after other races embraced Christianity. It was inspired by a desire to belong and was also caused by racism, especially in later times (Aylmer von Fleischer, *How Jesus Christ became White*).

THE REAL BLACK PANTHER

The real Black Panther, HADJ THAMI EL-GLAOUI AND LORD, head (Pasha) of the (Black Panther) Berber Clan until his death 1956. The Black Panther organization has been around for over two thousand years. There have been many heroes from Africa that the White people proclaim as their heroes in a White image: Hercules, Jesus, Moses, King Cephus (King Cephus is my direct ancestor), Hannibal, and now the Black Panther. Jesus's father was a Black Panther. Today the movie you are about to see is fiction, but at least cast the Black Panther in Black image. The Pasha, who is said to be the most powerful native figure in Morocco today, possesses the highest decorations and orders. Glaoui wears the grand cross of the legion of honor.

THE UNKNOWN TRUTH ABOUT THANKSGIVING

Thanksgiving is a day of conventional manifestation of sorrow for their ancestors among the Indian, starting in the 1300s through 1600s the white Europeans very survival was at the teaching and learning of the Wampanoag (Black) Indians, Native Americans. The white people came to America, into one of the Indian Villages, estimated 72,000 to 90,000 people living in South New England before contact with white Europeans. One hundred years later, the number was reduced by 80 percent, suffering from smallpox, typhus, measles, and other European diseases brought to this American continent. The Native Indians had no immunity, and some groups were totally wiped out.

Pilgrims arrived in the New World, America, during the winter, making it very difficult for them to find food and build shelter. Already weakened from their two-month voyage, most of the passengers failed to survive the first few months in their new home.

Fortunately, the native people, Indians called Wampanoag, already living in the Massachusetts Bay area, shared their knowledge of local crops and navigation with the Whites and helped the colonists survive.

White people gave their real thanks by sneaking into the Indians' villages before sunrise and massacred them. Infants were torn from their mothers' breast and hacked into pieces. The heads of the parents were chopped off, and little White kids kicked the heads around in the streets. Governor Bradford wrote, "It was a fearful sight to see them heads frying in the fire."

Affront of deceit to celebrate gratitude to the Indians and praise to God every third Thursday in November. The White people justification was that the Indians fail to fit into their lifestyle of civilization.

Today the holiday Thanksgiving has been whitewashed.

THE WHITE PEOPLE COPIED FROM AFRICA

Africa gave the White people everything they need to build their lives to where it is right now. Evidence: Those monuments called obelisks, stone pillars, typically having a rectangular cross section are symbols being blacked out through deceptive words or actions to cover up where they came from. Those monuments, symbols were first built in Africa thousands of years before the White people decided to erect a copy of it in Washington DC, USA. Isis (Eset), one of the most important deities (goddesses) of ancient Kemet of Africa, was married to her brother Osiris, but Seth, Osiris's brother, was jealous of him. Seth plotted and carried out the killing Osiris, cut him up in thirteen pieces and hid his body parts, scattered all over the land. Isis gathered a crew and searched everywhere for her husband's body parts and found all the parts, except his penis, then she created an artificial penis, and it was projected straight up in the air like a real penis. Thereafter, in memory of Osiris, his hard penis was as an obelisk monument in Black Africa for thousands of years before the White people copied it, putting it in Washington DC, USA. There are countless other things that the White people in general around the world have copied from Africa.

AMERICAN HISTORY CONTENT

Ruins of an Ancient Palengue Chiapas Mexico

THIRD EYE PINEAL GLAND

The pineal gland that activates the third eye is a small pine cone like gland. Every human being's gland can be activated into spiritual world frequencies that enables Black people to have a sense of their surroundings. The pineal gland can help you travel in other dimensions. This is also called astrotravel or remote viewing. With more advanced ancient practice, it is also possible to control thoughts and actions of other people of the world. Ancient societies like Kemet of Africa knew about the pineal gland. The pineal gland (third eye) is also on the back of the US dollar bill. People of the world, right now, have been doing research on the pineal for years, possibly to control what people are thinking in the world. While the physical eye sees the physical world, the third eye can see the true world; clear, unified, whole. you must learn to activate high-frequency energy. Activating high-frequency energies improves your health. Having low-frequency energies deteriorates your health. A healthy human body's frequency rate is 62-78 MHz. Having low or below 62 MHz frequency rate your body becomes subject to sickness. At 25 Mhz, the human body is subject to high death rate. Sunlight can stimulate the pineal gland to activate and produce hormones for the body. A healthy pineal gland gives power to your physical, mental, emotional, and spiritual life. The pineal gland uses the sun, music, X-rays, and many other energies, including nuclear and sound waves, to collect messages. Let me caution Black people in general to be careful; the USA government knows about this special power. They are studying it right now. To control you, Black people, they are putting chemicals in food, water chloride in toothpaste, chlorine in water, and brainwashing to calcify the pineal gland. Once the pineal gland is shut down, your ability to use your third eye disappears. When the pineal gland stops working properly, your abilities are reduced. *People of Africa have known about the third eye for thousands of years before Europe became aware of it. The third eye (pineal gland) gives you power. It produces melanin. Melanin is responsible for your physical, mental, emotional, and spiritual life. The blacker you are, the more melanin is in your body—the more power you got. Many secret society organizations know about this valuable information from Africa.*

THIS PICTURE IS SHOWING THE SYMBOL OF THE PINEAL GLAND

PICTURE CREATED BY JASPER

The pineal gland is found in the head, behind the eyes, just below. The pineal gland produces melanin, a biochemical that serves every functional part of the body, physical, mental, emotional, and spiritual life (Dr. Llaila Afrika, *Melanin: What Makes Black People Black!*). You can see that pineal symbol all around the world. Sometimes the pineal shape is found in buildings built, statues erected, and Christmas trees. The pineal gland is not a new science discovery; it has been known for thousands of years in Africa. Because of melanin, the pineal gland is called the master gland.

Melanin is the fundamental substance of the universe; it exists in cosmic, planetary, plant, and animal life. Melanin is black. Its chemical structures allow no energy to escape. It is the super absorber of energy: radiation, X-ray, music, sound, radar, radio waves, and sunlight wavelengths. Melanin is found in almost every organ of the human body, and it is necessary for the brain and nerves to operate, eyes to see, and cells to reproduce.

The Black human can energize their melanin from the pineal gland just by being in the sun or around the right type of music or sounds or other energy sources. Melanin itself, on a philosophical plane, is a black biochemical door through which the life force of Africans' spirituality passes in, moving from physical and the spiritual to material realm. The more Black you are, the more concentrated your melanin is.

TROGLODYTE NIGER (NIGGER)2

American content

The act or process of two or more genes combining different compounds, elements, or species, etc. The ancient Ibrida experiments were, in fact, ovum/zygote implant-combining genes into a uniform whole.

The two incongruent subjects of the Ibrida Experiments were

A. The human species (homo) Aboriginal/Oriental.
B. The (Anthropopethicus) Monkey/Ape, Zygote(s) (check dictionary) metrically genes combining in a uniform whole: A+B=C. Thus,
C. The Troglodyte Niger-Paleolithic man (hybrid) Occidental. (Ruddy- Pale Humanoid)

The resulting gene combining of the Ibrida experiments (C) was that of "ruddy pale" hairy humanoids, a synthetic man or android. These offsprings were, thereafter (under control environments), cross bred again and again with human cell produced by the union of two gametes, before it undergoes cleavage until a perfected form was manifest. This modern person today, we call him a White person, is the result of a Black scientist's experiments thousands of years ago. Experimentally-created manifest (or kind of person) is what had since been called mankind as opposed to man. Thus, the genesis of a "new" kind of man appeared on the planet. And this is the scientific truth about the genetic creation of modern man appearing on the planet.

TROGLODYTE NIGER

When one researches the words "Negro" and "nigger," by the Moor scientist, scientifically, genetically, or linguistically, what do facts reveal? Who or what genealogy or having the same ancestry related by same blood history and makeup are you researching? What is the true linguistic and biogenetic (production of living organisms from another living organism) categorization and classification of the words "Negro" and "nigger"? The truth (about the nigger) has much to do with ancient genetic research technology and experimentatio carried out in the Yucatan Peninsula at Mexico (mehoco) of Central Amexem/Africa and executed also in Patagonia. A core aspect of these ancient experiments had to with cross-ovum, cross-blood, and cross-gene, hetero-to-homo-perfection manifests. These scientific hurtles were accomplished at Patagonia of Southwest Amexem by the ancient Moabites/Moors. The Anthropithecus (troglodyte Niger) was at the center of one particular biogenetic, heterogenous aspect and was part of a broader range of Ibrida experimentation and research. Such experiments also involved hybrid corn, cell regeneration, hybrid food stock, herbs, enzymes, plant-life hybrids, etc. This serves to enhance certain positive qualities and improved plant cells resistance for variable fungi and disease, etc. The same was done with animals experimentally producing pig, chicken, and mule and Paleolithic (paleface/troglodyte Niger).

Think about it like this: Why is that Black people have over two hundred thousand years of civilized history, but the White people have only fifteen hundred years of civilized history? Where did they come from? The answer is in troglodyte Niger research.

TROGLODYTE NIGER (CHIMPANZEE)$_0$

from *The Natural History of Monkeys*, Sir William Jardine (Edinburgh, 1833).

There are piles of information about troglodyte Niger; opinions are not necessarily my own. I can, at best, give you an insight to the truth about history.

Heterogeneous (having a foreign origin) is the scientific opposite of homogeneous and means diverse of kind and nature, composed of completely different characters; incongruous (out of place) and foreign; being composed of diverse elements or constituents and not homogeneous; the crossing or blending of two different, unalike species. An example of heterogeneous would be A+B=C. Therefore, a mule is heterogenous, being a sterile hybrid of a male jackass (donkey) and a female horse. A seed cross with another seed, not of its own origin, produces a "hybrid."

Monkey or ape is homogeneous in its natural state. A man is homogeneous in his natural state. Cross the genes of the two male ape with the Black African female and the result is the Paleolithic troglodyte Niger, a hybrid.

TROGLODYTE NIGER (NIGGER) DISEASE AND REJECTION

A period of inter-socialization between the natural-hue people (original "hue" man) with the humanoid (man-kind) logically brought about curiosity, some intermixing, and (in many other instances) out and out fighting and rejection of the troglodytes. Interfacing among the natural-hue people, under less-controlled environmental conditions, produced an unexpected state of affairs and a series of unforeseen consequences. Among other identified consequences were that of wars, Niger (troglodyte) rejection, abnormal subjectivity and withdrawal among some Ibrida, linguistic confusion, general disorder, and of course, disease. The hybrids also attract lice (*Anoplura*), and their sebaceous (nature of glands) produce pungent odors. Distress began to creep into the once peaceful societies of the Moabite indigents of central and southwest. Aside from the logistical problems created by intense education and socialization, new, uncharted disease appears from among the true nigger (which is the Paleolithic troglodyte, "White man") to infect the populace. The identified strains that predominated the scientists' concern were these: gonorrhea, syphilis, and tuberculosis.

TROGLODYTE NIGER (NIGGER)

The "nigger problem" is unique in that it is a paradoxical intersocial deviation from the common rule of interfacing with humans (resembling human beings but not human), featuring their depraved, false belief activities. which have been misclassified as "racism". The truth about, and the root of, the nigger problems is genocidal polelithic (paleface) and birthright thief. This antisocial behavior negatively affects aboriginal (naturally by the law of nature) and indigenous societies as a whole. The nigger problem as an issue affecting a way of life, socially, politically, morally, ethically, economically, and spiritually. It manifests as injury (most specifically) to the suppressed Asiatics of Northwest Amexem, Northwest Africa, North America, who have been falsely branded as Negroes, Blacks, colored, Afro/ African, American West Indians, niggers, etc.

All those inappropriate names were coined by the *heterogenous* (its source or origin is outside the organism) to describe a civilly-lost, civilly-dead, and fallen hue people (dark hue/dark-skinned), who are descendants of a much greater culture, having extraordinary standards for higher knowledge. For those among us who think that we are really particularly coined names, challenge yourselves with some actual studies and research of two hundred thousand years of civilized Black history! Then ask yourselves how ridiculous we must have appeared to others from around the world. It is foul and vain for a person or a people to hold on to a lie when the truth has been revealed to them. *Troglodyte Niger is a crossbreed of an ape and a Black female who is not man but is man-kind.*

TROGLODYTE NIGER (NIGGER)

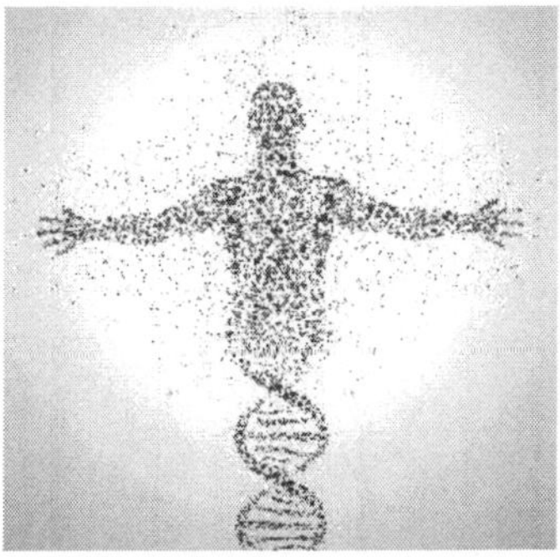

The truth, ptcede, the biggest lies, deceit, and human violation, when the white people hide and destroyed Black history. Simple truth: Troglodyte Niger is not a human, not a natural inhabitant of the earth. It cannot enjoy many things that the nature have put here for the human. The world is sick from living with false belief (miscreant). Black scientists produced the troglodyte Niger (nigger) thousands of yours ago through ancient genetic research technology by crossbreeding species (ape with Black female), and the result produced is a white humanoid (paleface, White people), resembling humans. The dark-hue/ dark-skinned natural peoples are the original human beings by the laws of nature, unlike the Paleolithic (paleface). There were other species produced by African scientists.

TROGLODYTE NIGERS (NIGGERS)

African scientists from Northwest Amexem, Africa, laboratories had produced the paleface humanoid, today known as the White people. In short, decisions were made to do all that was possible to solve the troglodyte Niger skin (cancer) problem and to cure diseases (gonorrhea, syphilis, tuberculosis). This unnatural paleface kind of man needed protection from the unforgiving among the natural-hue people yet to a more serious degree, from the equator sun, which appeared to cause lesions and cancers among the Paleolithic (humanoids) at an alarmingly rate. A more compatible environment was in order! Europe's weather patterns are unpredictable and changeable. Most of the time the temperatures in the area are more mild than on the Central America continent. Winter temperatures rarely drop below 32 degrees. Therefore, freezing is uncommon. Summers are generally mild, rarely rise above 90 degrees. Under these conditions, albo (albino) Paleolithic's would have a better chance at surviving the sun's heat insensitivity and could evolve to a higher state of civilize culture over time. England in Europe was the suitable place for the conditions for the Paleolithics (humanoids).

TROGLODYTE NIGER

Today humans (the original natural-hue people; aboriginal hue: brown, dark, black-skinned) realized that the humanoids/Paleolithics are different. They don't know the history of where they came from, are destructive, and have social disorder tendencies. Humanoids tend to be misunderstood and misclassified partly because people are not aware of the Europeans' origin. These intersocials do not quite fit in with nature, distorting proper names of people, places, things, and ideas. As this ancient anthropological history is revealed and reintroduced back to the original natural-hue peoples, their blind beliefs and misconceptions about history, philosophy, religion, geography, anthropology, grammar, and sociology, etc., (on a massive scale) will definitely change forever.

Knowing who you are definitely explains who the humanoids (man-kind, not man) really are.

ABANDONMENT OF OLD AMEXEM2

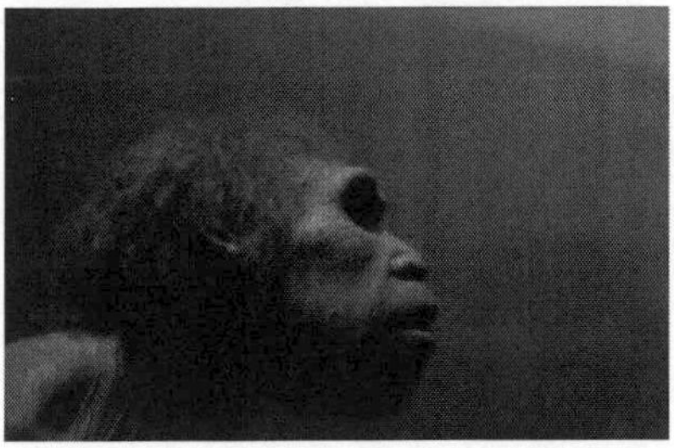

With the ancient laboratory complexes destroyed or burned, the Paleolithic issue became the scourge of the Yucatan and Mehecu. Many cities were shut down and abandoned, left to rot and decay! Among many, even the mention of the ancient experiment was taboo! Other aboriginals who had cohabitated with the Paleolithic Niger/nigger/Negro, were scorned and summarily cast as inferior and as beasts or animals, even though they did not show any direct relationship to the Ibrida nature other than a lighter complexion and somewhat more flaxen hair. And so it came to be that almost nobody would accept or openly be seen with the paleface Nigers/ Negroes (niggers). Others will mock the albo (albino), hybrids, calling them names, such as paleface, red dogs, etc. On the other hand, others were far more sympathetic, having created bonds or relationships. After all, our scientists initiated the experiments and carried them to fruition! *We made them!* Their Niger/Negro (nigger) problems were and still are our problems!

Today the White people are known as troglodyte Nigers, unnatural here on earth.

WERE THE FIRST JAPANESE BLACK PEOPLE?

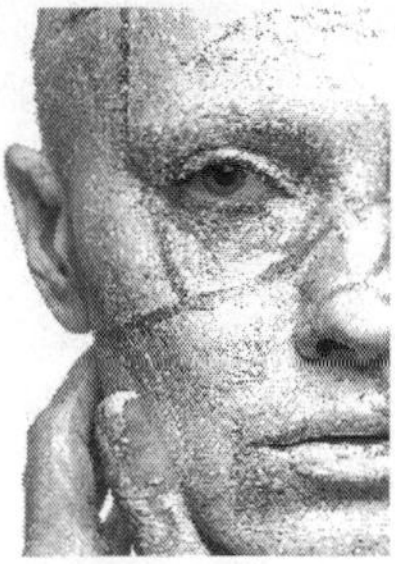

There is still evident Black strain in a certain element of the Japanese population, particularly those of the south. Imbert says, "The Black people element in Japan is recognizable by the Black aspect of certain inhabitants with dark and often Blackish skin, frizzly or curly hair. The Black people are the oldest race of the Far East. It has been proved that they once lived in Eastern and southern China as well as in Japan where the Black element is recognizable still in the population."

Professor Munro, one of the foremost students of Japanese life and culture, says, "The Japanese are a mixture of several distinct stocks. Black Mongolian . . . breadth of face, intraorbital width, flat nose, prognathism and brachycephaly (short-headed) might traced to Black African stock."

WEST AFRICA TRADE WITH THE AMERICAS

West Africa trade in the Americas increased because of the conflict in the Mediterranean.

The flourishing of the Olmec civilization occurred between 1500 BC and 1000 BC, when over twenty-two colossal heads of basalt, representing the West Africa Nigritic racial type, were carved. Olmecs traded rubber and other commodities with West Africa. They traveled in ancient seagoing vessels

WHITE JESUS WAS NECESSARY TO RULE THE WORLD

There was a time all Hebrews and Christian were Black humans until White people were converted. Previously, White Romans worshipped pagan deities and believed that the emperors were their gods. White people tried to kill and destroy the history of all Black Hebrews and Christians. Black Christians were murdered, fed to the lions for entertainment by the White Romans because the Black human "martyred." White people destroyed the history, art, and statues of Africans in Europe and Africa. White people had no history then. They began restoring Black history and culture in White images, claiming all science and religion were created by White people. Romans and the others later adopted Christianity and joined the ranks of the Black Christians, then other images of Jesus and his disciples began to take on non-Black features. This was because White Christians imagined Jesus, who had lived a long time ago, to be like themselves.

White people were not Christians at first; it was not until Emperor Constantine was converted to Christianity when it slowly began to make some positive enrolment in the religious lives of the Romans. Apollonius of Tyana (his picture above) was an idealist who represented the highest consciousness. He regarded himself as being appointed by god. White people call him a White Jesus today. There are many images of Jesus today, but they are all White. Around the world, There is no mistake that the true color of Jesus is in the Bible. Read it. White Christians who learn from the Bible ignore the truth.

WHITE SLAVES COME HOME

Many Black Americans still suffer from slavery of their ancestors in the USA. It happened too that while White Europeans and White Americans were raiding Africa for slaves, Africans were raiding the coast of Europe as far north as Sweden and Finland for slaves and had been doing it for ten thousand years. Evidence on this is abundant and indisputable. Collections were taken up in churches of the Europeans for ransom for some of those slaves. Ordre de Trinitaires was founded for that purpose.

The great White slave market was in Salee and Timbuktu of Morocco.

WHITES ARE IN "ILLUSIONS OF GREATNESS" BY FALSE HISTORY, THANKS TO DR. DOROTHY FARDAN

Whites have committed a grand theft and massive coverup of true history.

This coverup keeps most White Americans ignorant of the truth about themselves! In Yakub and the Origins of White Supremacy: Message to the White Man and Woman in America, Dr. Dorothy Fardan, a White member of the nation of Islam, writes, "This ignorance and rejection of history allows whites to continue in illusions of greatness and white supremacy that can only be eliminated by unfolding the layer of rejected history. What most white people fail to understand is that they too have been denied access to the true history which undergirds their present life, and in the absence of truth fail to gain knowledge of themselves. In rejecting Black history . . . they have rejected the truth of themselves and the crucial key to unlocking the doors to both the past and present, and therefore, any clear path towards the future."

Speaking on how Whites are trapped in a false history they do not understand, she continues, "What history are Caucasians trapped in then? It is a historical vacuum, a chunk of time which has been severed from its original point and reconstructed in term of fabricated accounts and falsified documents. Such a historical and truncated worldview has allowed the illusion of white supremacy to become not only a general mindset, but also an insidious underlying strategy which informs and constitutes every institution within American society. This mindset, which has no grounding in the origins of human presence, no recognized connection to be the first civilizations of human beings nor the wisdom accumulated in those civilizations (except for what was stolen and/or rethought and rewritten), is a mindset trapped. While the Europeans took what they needed and wanted from the original people in Africa to form the foundations of Western civilization, they simultaneously denied and rejected that very source. What occurred was a deliberate effort to cover up, conceal, and alter the true origins of human life in order to establish a supremacist worldview and eventually a civilization which recognized no liability for or answerability to the laws of nature embedded in the universe as well as in human nature."

WHITES HAVE DONE TO "ORIGINAL CHRISTIANITY" WHAT THEY HAVE DON TO TRUE BLACK HISTORY

The White man's Christianity is false Christianity! The original Christianity of the original Christians and the original biblical books has been greatly changed, distorted, censored, and reconstructed by Whites into a false Christianity, which served as a "weapon" and primary pillar of global White supremacy.

Major altering and censoring of biblical books were accomplished at the Council of Nicea in AD 325. In addition, whole books were deleted from the Bible. Evidence of missing biblical books exists within the Bible itself! These included the books of Jasher, Nathan, Shemaiah, Iddo, and Jehu, referred to in Nehemiah 21:14, Joshua 10:13, 2 Samuel 1:18, 1 Chronicles 29:29, and 2 Chronicles 9:29, 12:15, 20:34. The Bible, in its original form, was the product of African people. Though it has been greatly "messed" with by Whites, much truth is still available when you know true history.

YAKUB AL MANSUR, GREATEST OF THE (BLACK) MOORISH RULERS OF SPAIN (AD 1149-1199), J. A. ROGERS "THE WORLD'S GREAT MEN OF COLOR"

Yakub ibn Yusuf, better known as Al Mansur, was the ablest and most powerful of the Moorish rulers who dominated Spain for five hundred years. He was also one of the most enlightened, most just, and magnanimous. His surname, Al Mansur, means "the invincible." This was no braggadocio. He defeated all his enemies and never lost a battle.

Like nearly all the rulers of Morocco of Africa, he was Black. His father Yusuf was of Black ancestry, and his mother was unmixed Black woman from Timbuktu or Senegal.

Mansur came to power when his father was killed while besieging Santarem, Portugal, in 1184. He swore a great oath of revenge for his father's death. He gathered an army for the invasion of Spain and Portugal, and in 1889, with ten thousand of his redoubtable cavalry and foot soldiers, he landed at Algeciras, Spain. Marching on Santarem, Portugal, the scene of his father's death, he destroyed it, and then he continued to Lisbon and captured it. He returned to Africa laden with spoils and Christian captives, three thousand of whom were young women and children. On his return, there he was, stricken with fever, and the Christians in Spain, thinking the time propitious, gathered an immense army, aided by the crusaders, to drive the Moors out of the peninsula once and for all. The three principal leaders were Alphonso IX, King of Leon, in supreme command; Alphonso III of Castile; and Sancho I of Portugal. The Christians, winning victory after victory, neared Algeciras on the Mediterranean.

Alphonso, feeling certain that the Moorish rule was now at its end in Spain, sent a message of defiance to Mansur. "If it is too difficult for you to come to Spain," taunted Alphonso, "send me enough ships, and I will come to Africa to beat you there."

Mansur recruited people from the African Atlantic across to the border of Egypt of Africa. They came in all races, vast numbers, and of all color. In 1192, Mansur sailed from Alcassar and landed at Algeciras, Spain

Alphonso, with an army of three hundred thousand, one of the fastest ever assembled at that time, awaited Mansur near the fortress of Alarcos on the plains of Zalacs in 1086.

Mansur, as did Yusuf before him, resulted to strategy. Feeling sure Alphonso was going to direct his chief attack on that part of the Moorish army, where the royal standards were (since that was where Mansur would be), he shifted another commander, his uncle, to that place and went off to another. He also placed a number of his men in a position to cut off the retreat of a possible Christian force coming toward the royal standards.

Alphonso did exactly what Mansur had expected. Selecting ten thousand of the elite of his knights, he gave them the honor of drawing first blood and bringing Mansur a captive. Encased in their bright armor and mounted mettlesome horses, lances set, they swept down on the Moors. But Mansur's men stood firm and closing in on the Christian knights, hamstrung their horses and cut the riders to pieces. Alphonso, to have them, gave the order for a general advance, and his vast army swept down on the foe, the beat of his drums and the tramp of his men and horses shaking the ground like an earthquake. But again, the Moors held their ground and fought back with incredible fury and fanaticism, shouting, "There is no other God but God, and Mohamet is his prophet! God, alone, is invincible!" Alphonso, wounded, fled to Toledo. The surviving noblemen of his army surrendered to Mansur.

The number of Christians slain was immense. The estimate varies. Some historians say 30,000; others as high as 146,000. As for the spoils, some authors say 158,000 tents, 80,000 horses, 100,000 mules, 400,000 asses, and 60,000 suits of armor, *while the money and the jewels were beyond calculation*. Mansur reserved 5 percent of the booty for himself and gave the rest to his men.

Mansur went to Salamanca and Toledo, where Alphonso and his family had taken refuge. Cutting off all water and supplies from Toledo, Mansur was about to destroy the city when Alphonso's mother, wife, and children, with tears in their eyes, came to Mansur's lines to beg for mercy. Mansur, generous, always, not only granted their request but also sent them back laden with rich presents, and he set twenty-four thousand prisoners free.

REFERENCES

J. A. Rogers "Vol. 1,2,3 "World Great Men of Color" Vol. 1 "B.C. to A.D., Vol. 2 "3000 B.C. to 1946 A.D.," African Gift to America", and "Tutankhomen Tomb"

Afrika, Llaila. *Melanin: What Makes Black People Black!*

Basden, George Thomas. *Among the Ibos of Nigeria.*

M'Bantu, Anu. *Afro Hair of the Ancient Egyptians.*

Mloba, Wunyabori O. *Mau Mau and Kenya.*

Nwosu, Uzoma. *Igbo Voices.*

Skloot, Rebecca. *The Immortal Life of Henrietta Lacks.*

Suzar. *Blacked Out through Whitewash.*

Winters, Clyde. *African Empires in Ancient America.*